365 DAYS FOR HOPE

365 DAYS FOR HOPE

Daily inspiration for cancer patients!

By Ronald J. Avery

XULON PRESS

Xulon Press
2301 Lucien Way #415
Maitland, FL 32751
407.339.4217
www.xulonpress.com

© 2018 by Ronald J. Avery

Cover photo by Chuck Avery, Minneapolis, Minnesota

All rights reserved solely by the author. The author guarantees all contents are original and do not infringe upon the legal rights of any other person or work. No part of this book may be reproduced in any form without the permission of the author. The views expressed in this book are not necessarily those of the publisher.

Unless otherwise indicated,Scripture quotations taken from the Holy Bible, New International Version (NIV). Copyright © 1973, 1978, 1984, 2011 by Biblica, Inc.™. Used by permission. All rights reserved.

Printed in the United States of America.

ISBN-13: 978-1-54563-5-568

This book is dedicated to the lives, memories, and legacies of James D. Avery and Julie M. Avery.

They are the motivation for this book. We miss them daily but know that they are with us.

Foreword
by Bobby N. Koneru, MD

Cancer affects all of us. We know mothers, fathers, sons, daughters, and friends who have been diagnosed with the disease. As a radiation oncologist, I have been treating cancer patients for over 15 years. My patients continue to inspire me as they navigate through a long and arduous course of numerous doctors, tests, and treatments. Many are lifted by their faith and loved ones, which bring meaning to their struggle. Victor Frankl, the late Austrian neurologist, psychiatrist, and Holocaust survivor once said, "Everything can be taken from a man but one thing: the last of human freedoms—to choose one's attitude in any given set of circumstances, to choose one's own way." During the Holocaust, Frankl lost his wife and entire family. His famous book, *Man's Search for Meaning,* tells the story of how he survived the Holocaust, while many others who were physically stronger didn't survive. He attributes this to possessing an inner weapon: personal meaning for his experience. He proved that for even the most senseless and horrific circumstances, we can still find meaning and inspiration to persevere.

Sometimes we don't always understand the meaning of things, unless we lookback and connect the dots. One day I was looking at a historical building in the Millwork District of Dubuque, Iowa. As soon as I walked inside, I fell in love and I could see that the previous owner did as well. I ended up purchasing the building and later learned that it belonged to the late Jim Avery, who passed from colon cancer. This connection then led me to Ron Avery, his brother. Ron has sincerely been a champion for cancer patients. He started the Avery Foundation, a non-profit organization that provides valuable resources for patients who are financially in need. His book, *365 Days of Hope,* provides patients with daily insights and inspiration. The daily and weekly grind of treatments, diagnostic tests, and clinic visits can put anyone into an altered state that is not always optimal. For cancer patients, having this book can be a needed reminder for hope and meaning as they navigate through their journey.

Dr. Bobby Koneru is a TEDx speaker, radiation oncologist, and author of Confessions of a Radiation Oncologist. He is the founder of the Paramount Oncology Group, a radiation oncology organization that provides treatment and management services to community cancer centers, and co-founder of Cancer Fellows Foundation, an international non-profit organization that provides fellowships to radiation oncologists in-training. Dr. Koneru has been the keynote speaker for several national conferences and is a regular contributor to the Telegraph Herald.

Preface

I want to share the short biographies of Jim and Julie with you, so you know just a little bit about them. I will make mention of them often throughout this book. They are two incredible people who taught me many of life's valuable lessons. It still amazes me how they handled their journey with cancer with such courage and faith.

James Dale Avery was born on April 4, 1956 to Harvey and Mary Avery of Dubuque, Iowa, where he attended St. Patrick's School and Dubuque Senior High School. Jim was always interested in how mechanical things worked. At the age of ten, he was at his father's service station and found a box of motor parts in the backroom. After an hour, Harvey went to look for him only to find that Jim had put the motor completely back together and in working order.

Jim was self-taught on many things and was at the age to start to understand computers in their infancy into mainstream America. He went on to work for Cy-Care, a mainframe computer company in Dubuque, for many years. He later went on to start his own computer technology company. After he started to get bored with that work, he wanted to try something else. After a vacation to Italy, he fell in love with their ornamental railings. Upon his return to Dubuque, he started up Avery Railing Company in his garage. The company would soon outgrow his garage and move to the Millwork District of Dubuque. Many of the ornamental railings you see in Dubuque today can be traced back to Jim's handiwork at Avery Railing.

Jim lived his life to the fullest, doing what he wanted and when he wanted. He was a motorcycle enthusiast all his life. He was known to engage in daredevil stunts and assist the local daredevil, Jim McDermott. Jim once said he "lived a normal life" as one of his brothers was looking at a picture of Jim riding a motorcycle through a wall of fire. In January of 2014 he was diagnosed with stage 4 colon cancer. At that time the cancer had already spread to his liver, rectum, and bones. Jim continued to work for the next year and a half through his battle. Much of that time he was donating to help others, Voices, National Mississippi River Museum, and others. He also completed several inventions he was working on. One of those inventions winning an international award, the Avery Dicycle. He never stopped giving of himself.

Jim had the ability to see things in his mind and bring them to life. No directions, just his amazing vision. He was, in many ways, a true Renaissance man, in the spirit of Da Vinci. Jim wanted many of his tools and inventions to go to a maker's space where children could see, touch, use, and hopefully be inspired by them. On December 5, 2015, he passed away peacefully at home.

Relax

Life is way too short
Don't hide in your fort
Enjoy things of every sort
Life is there to court

So many things to see
Most good things are free
Be the best person you can be
Passing on glee has no fee

Stop to take the time
To see that everything is fine
Relax with a bottle of wine
With your valentine.

—Jim Avery, 2014

Julie Marie Avery was born on June 9, 1961 to Harvey and Mary Avery in Dubuque, Iowa. Julie attended St. Patrick's School, Dubuque Senior High, and the University of Northern Iowa. Julie was very active in school, track and field cheerleader,

Queen of the Tri-State Relays and a AFS foreign exchange student to Brazil, where she spent the summer of 1978.

In the spring of 1981, while home on break from the University of Northern Iowa, she developed pain in her upper thigh. Noticing how much pain she was in, Mary took her to a doctor. This first doctor told them that it was probably just a bruise. With the pain increasing, Mary took her to an orthopedic doctor. He immediately made arrangements for Julie to go straight to the hospital for an MRI. That MRI revealed a large tumor. The doctor suggested to Julie and Mary that they go to the Mayo Clinic in Rochester, Minnesota. He made appointments for Julie the next day there. Over the next three days of test after test, they were told that the tumor was cancer, fibrosis sarcoma. Because of the size and location of the tumor, Julie's leg had to be amputated. This surgery was originally scheduled for June 9, her 20th birthday. Julie asked not to have on her birthday and waited two more days.

Julie showed great courage through this. Keeping her spirits high, which helped our family through this. She was always more concerned for our well-being than of her own. She was determined that this cancer would not slow her down and keep her from living life. In the winter of 1981 she learned to ski with me at Sundown Mountain.

Preface

Julie, with one leg, was able to master the slopes before me. She also made a vacation trip to Los Angeles with her sister Cathy. In December she found a lump on her forehead and it was back to the Mayo Clinic right away. She started chemotherapy for this reoccurrence. By the spring of 1982 she was feeling well enough to travel, so she and I flew out to see our brother Mike in Princeton. During this visit she became very ill and was hospitalized for several weeks. When she had enough strength, we flew back to Dubuque. Once home, her and Mom went right to the Mayo Clinic. It was then the doctors told Julie and Mom there was nothing more they could do and she had maybe six months left.

Julie and Mom returned home, as Julie wanted to spend the remainder of her time at home with family. She spoke to each family member one on one to break the very sad news. Making sure we understood and that everything would be all right. Again, she was not concerned about her fate, she wanted us to understand and know that she would be fine if we were fine. On August 27, 1982 she passed away peacefully in her sleep with a smile on her face. The following poem she wrote for the family before she passed. This poem has been published several times.

The Circle

Life is time
Time captured
Time shared

An intersection of time
A brief union of space
Time shared?

Time captured?
I am your memories
You are my time

—Julie M. Avery, 1981

Introduction

We all know someone close or even yourself that have heard those dreadful words from the physician: "You have cancer." An almost instant shock falls onto the person. The mind starts racing 200 mph. One almost feels as though they were just dropped off onto a deserted island all alone. Questions upon questions race through the mind. Everything becomes a bit of a blur.

After all the dust has settled and the referral appointment to the oncologist has been made, one can start to come back to reality. The pain from the shock is still raw and will be for a while. It is during this time one must decide how they are going to proceed: with the fight and strength of a lion or the timidness of a baby lamb.

The following pages will give the cancer patient, who is the lion, a daily thought based from a famous quotation to help and inspire their journey with cancer for 365 days. You can read it one day at a time as intended, read it all at once, or start from anywhere in the book. Some topics will be mentioned several times, but from different avenues.

All topics meant to bring you uplifting support for the journey.

I was a very young man when I watched my dear sister Julie embark on the same journey. Watching her roller coaster ride was difficult at best. Thirty some years later, I witnessed the same journey, this time being captained by my beloved brother Jim. This journey had its rough seas as well. In my direct family, including both parents, we have had six out of ten of us receive those dreadful words. Four out of the six journeys ended with positive results. I also have had the unpleasant pleasure of helping a few friends and many former employees through this journey. Too many of us are having to make this journey! The goal of this book is to give the cancer patient a daily thought to make their journey a little brighter and a little smoother.

"We want to be a rainbow in cancer patient's stormy clouds!"

—Ronald J. Avery
Dubuque, Iowa
January 2018

Romans 12:12

Be joyful in hope, patient in affliction, faithful in prayer.

DAY 1

Cancer is a word, not a sentence.
—John Diamon, 1953-2001
British Journalist

Hopefully this is true for all cancer patients. When you receive your diagnosis, remember that it is just a word from our dictionary. Find the courage and strength within to fight that word and keep it from giving you a sentence. You need to stay in control of it. Don't let it control you. You will not be alone in this journey. You have family, friends, loved ones, and us to help you along the way. Lean on us when you need to. We will be there.

For some patients their diagnosis comes in bad, like it did for my brother Jim. Receiving a diagnosis stage 4 is never good. Especially when the physician tells you that you have 18-24 months to live. That very well sounds like a sentence and not a word. But don't let it be a sentence! It is still just a word!

When you keep it a word and control it, you will be amazed at what you can accomplish while on this journey. Jim was able to complete several inventions during this time and travel to some museums he wanted to see. Those inventions were gifted to a Makers Space in Dubuque, Iowa where his legacy will live on through those inventions as children and adults will learn from them. Keep it a word and make your legacy!

DAY 2

One ought never to turn one's back on a threatened danger and try to run away from it. If you do that, you will double the danger. But if you meet it promptly and without flinching, you will reduce the danger by half. Never run away from anything. Never!
—Winston Churchill, 1874-1965
British Prime Minister

I can just hear Churchill in his heavy English accent saying these words to rally the English people against the Nazi Germany war machine. If your team was down by 50 points at halftime and the coach brought in Winston Churchill to talk to the team, I am sure your team would rally in the second half and win! His words move people to action.

These words can be very meaningful for you as you start your journey with cancer. Don't turn your back on the cancer. Don't try to run away from it. If you do that, you give that cancer the opportunity to double its strength. Hold firm and meet it promptly. Do not flinch and give it all you have. Make the cancer flinch! Never run away!

DAY 3

Have no fear of moving into the unknown. Simply step out fearlessly knowing that I am with you, therefore no harm can befall you; all is very, very well. Do this in complete faith and confidence.

—Saint John Paul II, 1920-2005
Polish Pope of the Catholic Church

Do not let fear take up residency within you as you start your unknown journey. Your God is with you, along with all of us. So, you can be fearless taking your first steps on this journey. Have complete faith and confidence in yourself and in your God that no harm shall befall you.

I remember when my sister Julie started her journey at a very young age of 20. You would think she was full of fear entering her journey. She was not. She had such strong support from family and friends. Especially from Fr. Edward Petty, who spent many a day sitting on the patio with Julie talking about life and yes death. I know that his words gave Julie great faith and confidence that however her journey ended, no harm would befall her.

DAY 4

What you can do, or dream you can, begin it. Boldness has genius, power and magic in it.
—Johann Wolfgang Von Goethe, 1749-1832
German Poet

Be bold! Be bold in your fight against cancer. Be bold in how you live along this journey. Don't be afraid to begin a dream of yours and make it reality. Do not let cancer slow you down mentally or physically. On your bad days, with much pain and little strength, your boldness may be just a simple walk around the neighborhood. That boldness makes you genius, gives you power and magic. Your boldness does not have to be something so great as launching a rocket to the moon. For you and your journey it could be something that seems simple, but on that day, it is a rocket to the moon in your eyes.

Jim and Julie both traveled their journeys with this attitude. They were very bold. Julie traveled to east and west coast to see the Atlantic and Pacific

Oceans. She learned how to downhill ski after her leg was amputated. She could do it, she dreamed it, and she began it. She was magical! Jim did so much during his journey. Always stopping what he was doing to help his buddies with problems they could not solve and they knew he could. He did not only begin his dreams but aided his buddies in theirs. So, be bold! You will be surprised at what you can accomplish and surprised at the strength that it gives you.

DAY 5

A brave man is a man who dares to look the devil in the face and tell him he is a devil.
—James A. Garfield, 1831-1881
20th President of the United States

Be brave and stand eye to eye with your devil, cancer, and tell him he is the devil and does not belong here! You are brave! Do not let the evil beast think he has you backed into the corner. Stand toe to toe with him. By keeping this frame of mind, you will find that it gives you greater inner strength, which will allow you to get up tomorrow and do the same. This journey is not easy at all. You know that very well. Your bravery during this journey just may take some of the twists and turns out of it.

DAY 6

If you bring forth what is within you, what you bring forth will save you. If you do not bring forth what is within you, what you do not bring forth will destroy you.
—Jesus Christ
God's only begotten Son

Bring forth your best for this journey: positive attitude, faith, confidence, strength, hope, and love. This can save you. Do nothing and this journey will be short and have a sad ending. The positive attitude, faith, confidence, strength, hope, and love are all very good medicine for you. These are more powerful than any medicine that your physician will prescribe you. You must bring forth these "medicines" daily during your journey. Making this journey without them would be like taking a journey to Hawaii and not bringing your bathing suit, sunscreen, and sunglasses.

DAY 7

Surround yourself with good people. People who are going to be honest with you and look out for your best interest.
—Derek Jeter, 1974-present
American Professional Baseball Player

This is so very true for a cancer patient beginning their journey to battle cancer. These good people become key components to your army in this battle. They will be there for you when you need the straight and honest truth to stand and fight. They will always keep your best interest in mind while pushing straight ahead. They will be there to help you up when you fall down. They will give you the encouragement you need on the tough days. Their shoulders will hold up firm when you need to cry on them.

Jim and Julie had their circle of good people who were always there for them. Sometimes just as simple as stopping by and saying hello, taking them to lunch, remembering good old stories from earlier years and just being there with them. Those good people make for good medicine. They can turn a sour day for you into an afternoon of laughs and smiles. Gather your good people and let them know you will need them.

DAY 8

Your present circumstances don't determine where you can go; they merely determine where you start.
—Nido Qubein 1948-present
American Businessman

Your cancer does not determine where you are going. It is just a starting point on your journey. You, your physicians, your caretakers, your family, your friends, and your faith will determine where you are going. Never let the cancer take the lead and send you down a long, dark, and narrow road. The wheel is in your hands! You drive and let those around you guide you. Tell cancer this is your car. You're driving it where it needs to go.

DAY 9

There is nothing impossible to him who will try.
—Alexander the Great, 356 BC-323 BC
Greek King of Macedonia

When you set forth on this journey, it very well may seem impossible to overcome. It is not, if you try. If you keep a positive attitude, have faith, have courage, have a strong team around you, have determination, and never give up, you can do it. All of those make the impossible possible when working together like a fine oiled machine. Try, you must!

DAY 10

Never let a bad situation bring out the worst in you. Choose to stay positive and be the strong person that God created you to be.

—Unknown

Your situation with cancer is bad. Cancer of any kind or any stage is plain and simply bad. It is so very important not to let that cancer bring out the worst in you. Your mental state during this journey is very key to your success or your failure. Stay positive and strong during this journey. God made you strong and now is the time to show it.

So many cancer patients I have known—Jim, Julie, Dad, Mom, Chuck, Donna and many more—live up to this when they receive their diagnosis. Those people I mentioned are just immediate family members. If I listed everyone I knew, this would be a very long book. Let that bad situation start a fire within you! You cannot change the diagnosis, but with the right attitude and your strength, you can beat it. We hope all of us can be like that when forced into a corner.

DAY 11

All adventures, especially into new territory, are scary.
—Sally Ride, 1951-2012
American Physicist & Astronaut

Your adventure into this new territory of cancer is, of course, scary. Remember that you are not an astronaut alone on a space mission. Just as Sally did when she became the first female in space on the shuttle Challenger, she had a great team of support with her on board and a great team at mission control. You will have a great team around you. Think of your family, friends, and loved ones as your fellow astronauts. With you every day to keep you pushing forward, for you to lean on, for you to cry to, for you to smile and laugh with. Consider your physicians, nurses, and caretakers as your mission control. They will help guide you on this journey, so you don't go astray. They will be your technical guides during this journey. With this great support, there is no need to be scared. Set forth with confidence.

DAY 12

A clear vision, backed by definite plans, gives you a tremendous feeling of confidence and personal power.
—Stanley Stans, present Kenyan Motivational Author

As mentioned in our thought from yesterday, mission control—your physicians, nurses and caretakers—will be your guide on this journey. They will lay out the vision of your journey with definite plans. If you have any uncertainty or questions, you must ask! Make sure you are clear on this vision. Make sure you understand what exactly you need to do for the plans. You also need to know what everyone's role is on your team. Knowing all of this will give you the confidence you need to look at cancer right in the face and say, "Not on my watch!" You will be empowered to beat that evil beast down. Without a clear vision and definite plans, it would be like being dropped in the middle of some strange land blindfolded and told to find your way home. Your confidence and personal power would be next to zero. Now if you are dropped off in a strange land with a GPS unit, maps, food, money, and no blindfold, your confidence and personal power would be great. You would be very confident that you could make your way home. Make sure you have a clear vision and definite plans. Your journey will be less troublesome.

DAY 13

Optimism is the faith that leads to achievement. Nothing can be done without hope and confidence.
—Helen Keller, 1880-1968
American Author & Activist

It's hard to have optimism when you have just been told you have cancer. One needs to think as the glass is half full, not half empty. Without optimism, it will be very hard to have the achievement of beating cancer. Your mental state is very much the key to the success you will have on this journey. That optimism, that faith will pull you up each day and give you the strength to fight on. Each day that optimism and faith grow, it gives you more hope and more confidence. You don't go to battle with no weapons and think you are going to win. Consider optimism as your body armour, faith as your sword, hope as your helmet, and confidence as your great white stallion. Now you are ready to battle the evil beast.

DAY 14

A great attitude becomes a great day, which becomes a great month, which becomes a great year, which becomes a great life.
—Mandy Hale, 1978-present
American Author

Think of your attitude as the seeds you plant in your garden in the spring. You plant them and water them and you feel great. It's a great day. During the first month, you watch closely as they sprout up from the earth. You take great care with them. Making sure they get the water they need and the weeds stay away. You continue to take care great of them throughout the summer as they grow into sturdy plants, bearing fruit. You keep them free from weeds and bugs. They always have water they need. It has become a great growing year, bearing fruits to give you a great life. If you let your attitude slip and you don't care and don't nurture it, the plants will struggle to grow. The days become hard. The weeds and bugs attack the plants, making for long summer months for them. Come harvest time, those plants have been over taken by the weeds and bugs and bear no fruit. The growing year is a bust and life becomes hard without fruits to nurture you. You must constantly care for attitude. Keep it in check and positive. Do not let the weeds and bugs, cancer, get to it. Give your attitude plenty of water and sunlight to grow and blossom. Your great days will lead to great months, which will lead to a great year, which will lead to a great life cancer-free because you maintained a great attitude and kept it nurtured.

DAY 15

We must embrace pain and burn it as fuel for our journey.
     —Kenji Miyazawa, 1896-1933
         Japanese Poet

Hearing the words "embrace pain" would be difficult for anyone. Especially for cancer patients who endure pain daily. Let that pain become nice, dry firewood that you are going to burn for your fuel and strength for the journey at hand. Each time you feel that pain, grab it like firewood and throw it on your fire. Saying to yourself, "Not today, cancer pain! You just gave me more resolve and strength to fight you off." Embrace the pain and burn deep within you. Giving you the strength each day to fight. Knowing that someday your firewood pile will run empty just like your cancer and your journey will be complete.

DAY 16

We don't even know how strong we are until we are forced to bring that hidden strength forward. In times of tragedy, of war, of necessity, people do amazing things. The human capacity for survival and renewal is awesome.
—Isabel Allende, 1942-present
Chilean-American Writer

You will be forced to bring out your hidden strength in your time of tragedy: cancer diagnosis. You don't know it now, but you will know it soon just how strong you are and the amazing things you will do to survive. We all have heard of those amazing stories of people's lives being saved by the unknown strength of another person. Like a car falling off its jack and crushing the mechanic under it. Another mechanic comes to the rescue and somehow gathers the strength to lift the car up far enough for the injured to slide out. You hear stories like this all the time. That hidden strength is in all of us because we have great capacity for survival and renewal. Now is the time for you to call upon your hidden strength, so you can survive this cancer and be renewed.

I remember being so amazed at my sister Julie and her strength throughout her journey. She was by far the strongest 100-pound female you ever met. She brought forth her hidden strength day after day. Her greatest strength was making sure her little brother understood what was going on and that all would be good, no matter the outcome. Her strength was absorbed into me. Without her strength and guidance, I know that her death would have affected me negatively. So, when you bring your hidden strength forward, know that it is also helping the loved ones around you.

DAY 17

You can beat cancer by how you live, why you live, and in the manner in which you live.
—Stuart Scott, 1965-2015
American Sportscaster

Great words of wisdom from a good man that was taken too early. Live your life to the fullest. How you live: with a positive attitude, with strong faith, with hope, with courage, with respect, with dignity, and with love of all others. Why you live: to serve others, not yourself, to help those in need, to teach the next generation, to leave this earth better than it was when you came into it. In the manner in which you live: knowing that we are all equal, that the color of our skin, the faith we practice, the gender we are, and our sexual orientation does not make us better than another. Live your life in a positive manner with a smile on your face. Open a door for someone. Help an elderly lady with her groceries. Say hello to people you meet. Do all those simple things that makes our daily lives better. Not only will you have a smile on your face, you will bring many more smiles to other faces. This is what I call good medicine for you. It makes you feel better, which in turn gives you more strength for your journey.

DAY 18

Courage is rightly esteemed the first of human qualities because it is the quality which guarantees all others.
—Winston Churchill, 1874-1965
British Prime Minister

Find your courage within you. It's there; don't think it isn't. Remember the cowardly lion in *The Wizard of Oz?* He had no courage. He was very shy and timid. Scared of every little thing. He couldn't fight his way out of a wet paper bag. He did know that he needed courage to be the King of the Jungle. He joined Dorthey, the Tinman, and the Scarecrow on their journey to see the Wizard down the yellow brick road. Their journey was filled with troublesome events with the witch and the flying monkeys. Much of those troublesome events could have been avoided if the cowardly lion had some courage. All does end good for the lion though, when they finally reach the Wizard of Oz and he is given courage. His chest puffs out and he has a deep roar of the King. Find your courage before you start your journey with cancer. The road will be less treacherous with courage in your back pocket. That courage will allow your other qualities to come forth as well: determination, faith, positive attitude, hope, love, and personal inner strength. All of which will make your journey smoother. Isn't it funny how Winston Churchill and the Wizard look alike? Both giving courage to many. So, on one of those bad days when your strength is weak and courage seems to have slipped away, sit down and watch *The Wizard of Oz* or listen to an old speech of Churchill's from World War II. Your courage and strength will come right back.

DAY 19

> *Sometimes life hits you in the head with a brick. Don't lose faith.*
> —Steve Jobs, 1955-2011
> American Business Magnate

You have been hit in the head with a brick, a brick of cancer. Don't let that brick knock your faith out of you. Don't ever lose faith in yourself; your physicians, nurses, caretakers, family and friends all have faith in you. Let their faith in you keep your own faith burning strong. You will have a lot of faith surrounding you. Lean on it, use it to help carry you throughout your whole journey.

Hebrews 11:1 tells us, *"Faith is the confidence that what we hope for will actually happen; it gives us assurance about things we cannot see."*

II Corinthians 5:7 states, *"For we walk by faith, not by sight."*

I Corinthians 16:13,14 also tells us, *"Be on guard; stand firm in faith; be courageous; be strong. Do everything in love."*

I Corinthians 13:13 gives us an important reason for three things we will talk a lot about in this book, *"Three things will last forever—faith, hope and love—and the greatest of these is love."*

You cannot overlook how important faith will be on your journey!

DAY 20

May the forces of evil become confused on the way to your house.
　　　　　—George Carlin, 1937-2008
　　　　　　　American Comedian

The problem for you is that the forces of evil, cancer, have already found your house. Now is the time for them to get confused and forget how long their stay at your house was supposed to be. Make it short and send them on their way. Do this by showing great courage, faith, hope, determination, and personal strength. When the forces of evil see all that coming at them, hopefully they run to the door to get away! Then shut and lock the door so they never return.

DAY 21

I had cancer; cancer never had me.
　　　　　—Emily Ransom, 1995-present
　　　　　　　　American Poet

This is such a great way to think about your cancer. Tell yourself this each morning. Keep control of your destiny. Never, ever let the evil beast get control of you. You have all the weapons you need to keep the beast from getting control. You have great physicians, nurses, caretakers, family, friends, loved ones, a clear vision of your plan, faith, hope, courage, love, determination, strength, and on and on. With all that, your confidence will never let cancer have you.

DAY 22

Life is not a solo act. It's a huge collaboration and we all need to assemble around us the people who care about us and support us in times of strife.
　　　　　　　　—Tim Gunn, 1953-present
　　　　　　　　American Fashion Consultant

You are in times of strife with your cancer. Your journey with it is no solo act, either. You need to assemble all the people you care for you, family, friends, and loved ones. You will need support on this journey. For it will not be easy. It will not be painless. The journey does not take you down a brightly lit eight-lane expressway. This journey will be down a dark and narrow road filled with twists, turns, and potholes. Those that you assemble will be your support during this time of strife. They will be the ones to fix the flat tire when you hit the pothole. They will be the ones to push you out of the mud on that dark road. They will be there to tell you, "Great job!" Their encouragement will be fuel for your vehicle. When you want to make a task simple, surround yourself with good people!

DAY 23

Don't defy the diagnosis; try to defy the verdict.
—Norman Cousins, 1915-1990
American Author

You cannot run away from the diagnosis, but you sure can defy the verdict. A diagnosis is just the identification of the nature of an illness. It is what is. What you need to concentrate on is how to rid yourself of that illness. Don't ever believe the diagnosis is the end-all. No, no never do that! You have the opportunity to determine the verdict of this illness. Stand firm with great courage and faith that you will do everything in your power to rid yourself from this. Never give up and never give in. All of us are here to help.

DAY 24

Play like a champion today!
—University of Notre Dame Football

365 Days for Hope

A champion is a person who has defeated or surpassed all rivals in a competition. Every home football game for the University of Notre Dame the players leave the locker room to head out onto the field. They go down a flight of stairs. Hanging on the wall at the bottom of this first flight is a sign that reads, "Play like a champion today!" Each player touches that sign on the way by to remind them to play like a champion that day, to defeat the rival. You have a big rival game every day: you vs. cancer. Cancer is your rival. Will you play like a champion each day to defeat this rival? Will you lift the championship trophy of cancer-freedom above your head for all to see? Yes, yes you can. You have assembled a championship caliber team of physicians, nurses, caretakers, family, friends, and loved ones. You have a great game plan. Now you must execute this plan daily. Giving it your best every day. Don't let your rival, cancer, see you blink.

DAY 25

The only disability in life is a bad attitude.
—Scott Hamilton, 1958-present
Olympic Gold Figure Skater

Scott knows very well the importance of a positive in life. You need it for everything, not just for difficult times. Do you think Scott could have made it to be a four-time U.S. Figure Skating Champion with a bad attitude? Do you think he could have won an Olympic Gold Medal with a bad attitude? Do you think Scott could get through his testicular cancer with a bad attitude? Do you think Scott could get through three bouts with benign brain tumors with a bad attitude? Your answer to all these questions is "NO!"

There is no place for a bad attitude on this journey of yours. A bad attitude for you would be like dragging a huge anchor behind as you try to move forward down the path of your journey. That thing will slow you down, way down. What happens when you slow down on this journey? Yes, the cancer catches up more and gives it more chances to do more damage. A bad attitude on this journey is very dangerous. Stay positive throughout and lean on your team when you need to. Stay the course. Keep pushing forward. Don't look back.

DAY 26

Life is not a matter of holding good cards, but of playing a poor hand well.
　　　　　—Robert Louis Stevenson, 1850-1894
　　　　　　　　　　　　　　Scottish Poet

Well, you have been dealt a very poor hand. How will you play it? The outcome of how you play your hand has much more meaning. It's "play the poor hand well and live another day" or "fold your hand and meet your creator". When I was young, my brother Bob, Julie, Mom, and Dad would play penny poker. We had such fun playing. We would play for hours and by the end of the night the big winner would win maybe $1.50. Julie was always the master, bluffing us. I almost always fell for her bluffs. She could play a bad hand right into the winning hand. She took the experience of those family night poker games and used them to play her bad hand life gave her, cancer, the best possible way she could. Believe me, she played like poker's grand champion. She will always be my champion!

DAY 27

Call it a clan, call it a network, call it a tribe, call it a family. Whatever you call it, whoever you are, you need one.
—Jane Howard, 1935-1996
American Journalist

It is so important to have "one" when you are the journey of battling cancer. I would call it my team. You will need it for comfort and encouragement, love and caring, for the good times and the bad times. Your team will be your rock. Your difficult journey cannot be made alone. Do not close them out. Let them in and lean on them to get you through.

DAY 28

If you're walking down the right path and you're willing to keep walking, eventually you'll make progress.
—Barack Obama, 1961-present
44th President of the United States

The first step is to make sure you are walking down the right path. President Obama made sure he was walking down the right path for his political career. His political career started as an Illinois State Senator in 1997. He served there until 2004 and then launched his campaign to be the U.S. Senator from Illinois. He delivered the keynote speech at the Democratic Convention that summer that led him to a landslide victory in November for the U.S. Senator seat. He gained national and international attention with his quick rise in the Democratic Party. President Obama stayed on that short path to take him to his party's nomination for President in 2008. He went on to win the election in November over John McCain to become the nation's first

African-American President. You need to follow the path that your physicians have mapped out for you. That path will not be easy, but it will be possible to reach its end. You must be willing to keep walking. Do not let the evil beast, cancer, distract you away from this path. Your willingness and determination to keep pushing ahead will bring you progress. Build on that progress daily. With any luck, your journey will be as short as President Obama's was to reach the ultimate goal.

DAY 29

Family is the most important thing in the world.
—Princess Diana, 1961-1997
Princess of Wales

Always, always keep your family close. They will be good medicine for you during this journey. They will be there to give you encouragement, love, support, time, and hope. All key elements you need for this journey. They will be there when you need a good cry and someone to listen to you. They will be there to share some laughter with you. They will be there simply to hold your hand some days.

When Julie began her journey with cancer in 1981 our family was not super close. We had family scattered across the country and did not see each other very much. As her journey went on, the closer our family became. Brothers and sisters from out of town made trips back to Dubuque to see Julie. Julie needed that, as did each of us. We all needed each other as her journey was coming to an end. The end we hoped and prayed would not happen. Thirty-four years later we were reminded how important family is when Jim started the same journey with cancer. We understood at that time, better than 1981, how much family could help on Jim's journey. We were blessed by having much more time together with Jim as a complete group during his journey. You could see the energy that it gave Jim when we were all together. There is *no* doubt on how important family is. Bring yours in close as you battle the evil beast.

DAY 30

Resolve never to quit, never to give up, no matter what the situation.
 —Jack Nicklaus, 1940-present
  American Professional Golfer

Have this resolve! There is always hope in any situation. You may have to look harder and deeper to find that hope, but it is there. Giving up should never be an option. Jack is the perfect example of this. He such great resolve, it made him the greatest golfer of all time. How else could you explain his record? He amassed 73 PGA Tour Victories, six Master Championships, five PGA Championships, four U.S. Open Championships, three British Open Championships, and three Players Championships. He also won eight Senior Major Championships. Oh yes, he also won two U.S. Amateur Championships. Another awesome number for Jack is 19 second place finishes in major tournaments. The greatest of his victories was the 1986 Masters, which is also known as the greatest moment in golf history. Jack was a chubby 46-year-old who was written off by many golf writers and other players. Instead of calling him Golden Bear, they were calling him Oldie Bear. Jack did not let any of that bother him. For Jack had his great resolve. When Jack reached the back nine on the final day he was four strokes behind the leader. This was the Masters; nobody could overcome that on this back nine. Nobody but the chubby 46-year-old, washed up oldie bear. This bear was still Golden as he played the back nine that day in 30 strokes! Completely unreal. The crowd roars from Augusta, Georgia could be heard all the way to the White House. Jack passed eight players on that back nine to win his final major, his greatest major, and golf's greatest major. That is what I call resolve!

If Jack can show such great resolve for a sport, a game, I think you can muster up some great resolve to fight cancer. Yours has much more meaning. For you, this is not a game; it is life or death.

DAY 31

We will not waiver; we will not tire; we will not falter, and we will not fail. Peace and freedom will prevail.
—George W. Bush, 1946-present
43rd President of the United States

President Bush used these words to help heal our nation after the 9/11 attacks. These words can be very useful after your attack from cancer. Do not waiver! Stay the course the physicians have laid out for you. Steady and straight ahead; there are no shortcuts. Do not waiver! Do not tire! Stand up and fight each day. Some days it will be very hard. On those days, small progress is good. Do not tire! Do no falter! Keep pushing forward. Lean on your support team to help you. Do not falter! Do not fail! Failure here is not an option. If you do pass on from cancer, it does not mean you failed! You did your best—you did not waiver, you did not tire, you did not falter—so you did not fail. Peace for you and freedom from cancer will prevail.

DAY 32

What cancer cannot do. Cancer is so limited... It cannot cripple love, it cannot shatter hope, it cannot corrode faith, it cannot destroy peace, it cannot kill friendship, it cannot suppress memories, it cannot silence courage, it cannot invade the soul, it cannot steal eternal life, it cannot conquer the spirit.
—Robert L. Lynn, 1931-present
American Poet

When you read this, it should give you hope and encouragement. It is like a locker room pep talk to the team before they take the field. Can you picture yourself on locker room bench listening to these words from someone like Knute Rockne or Vince Lombardi? Getting you all fired up to go out there and kick cancer's butt. This would give you so much encouragement. Your attitude would soar. You would feel strength you thought you didn't have. Your confidence level would be at an all-time high. You can almost hear cancer shivering from fear.

Take these words and type them into a Word document and print it. Post it on your refrigerator so you can read them each and every day. It will be like breathing in the fresh morning air.

DAY 33

God grant me the serenity to accept the things I cannot change, the courage to change the things I can, and the wisdom to know the difference.
　　　　—Reinhold Niebuhr, 1892-1971
　　　　　　American Theologian

You have already shown great serenity in accepting your cancer diagnosis. Now you need to wear the badge of courage each day during your battle. Battling cancer would frighten anyone. Your ability to do so shows your courage. It shows your bravery, valor, fearlessness, nerve, daringness, boldness, true grit, gallantry, and moxie. It almost sounds like I am describing a superhero. Yes—yes, I am. Anyone that fights the battle against cancer is a superhero to me! With being the superhero you are, you have the wisdom to know the difference between accepting the things you cannot change and the courage to change the things you can.

DAY 34

The true competitors, though, are the ones who always plan to win.
　　　　　　—Tom Brady, 1977-present
　　　American Professional Football Player

As a cancer patient, you are a competitor in the game of life. No greater is a game than yours. None has more meaning than yours. Tom Brady is the truest of competitors. His personal records and his team records shout that very clearly. He is still playing quarterback in the NFL at the age of 40 and is in better physical shape than he was when he was a rookie. Nobody out prepares Tom. His plan is to win every game. Most games he does win. He has won five Super Bowl Titles, four Super Bowl MVPs, two NFL MVPs, 12 Pro Bowls and 14 Divisional Titles.

You are a true competitor and you have a plan to win that your physicians have laid out for you in a playbook for this all-important game. Prepare yourself for that playbook. Know exactly what you need to do. Believe in the playbook. Have the faith and confidence that this playbook will work. Make sure your team, physicians, nurses, caretakers, family, friends, and loved ones know the playbook as well. Now is the time to execute the playbook and take yourself to victory. A victory that means more than any of Tom Brady's Super Bowl Championships.

DAY 35

You always have two choices: your commitment versus your fear.
—Sammy Davis Jr., 1925-1990
American Actor & Singer

There is a lot of fear with cancer. Let's not kid ourselves and think there isn't. If someone tells you different, I want what they had for breakfast. You need to make it your choice that you are committed to beat down that fear and the cancer that brought that fear to life. Do not waiver. Do not look back. Straight ahead with confidence and conviction. Do not let fear try to work its way back in. We are committed to help you. To help you on this journey and to help keep your fear at bay.

DAY 36

I might have had a tough break, but I have an awful lot to live for.
—Lou Gehrig, 1903-1944
American Professional Baseball Player

I remember as a kid watching old baseball highlights and Lou Gehrig's speech at Yankee Stadium. I will never forget it. What grace he had to give that famous speech. Lou was looked to by many young kids as their Superman. He could do it all. Now their great superstar was telling the world he soon would die. What a man! Too bad our superstars today are not more like Lou Gehrig.

You caught a tough break as well with your cancer. You, too have an awful lot to live for. Never give up. Keep living your life and fulfilling your dreams as you battle the evil beast. Have the grace and class Lou had. Your journey may end on a much better note than Lou's. If it doesn't, know that you went out on top with grace and class.

Jim and I had a very good conversation shortly after he told us he had about 18-24 months to live. He had the same grace and class as Lou. I looked up to Jim as a young kid, as my hero. He rode motorcycles and did some stunts. This was the early 1970s, when Evel Knievel was huge. Well, Jim was my own personal Evel Knievel. The conversation we had brought memories of the Lou Gehrig speech and how his young fans felt. Jim, almost exactly like Lou, said, "Yes it sucks, but I have had a good life and have done what I've wanted to do." I was amazed by his acceptance and also proud. I asked about a bucket list and Jim said he has completed that list. My brother had the same Superman grace and class as Lou Gehrig. So, be willing to accept the outcome good or bad with grace and class. You will leave a great legacy doing so.

DAY 37

You just have to have simple faith.
—Jimmy Carter, 1924-present
39th President of the United States

These words from a man that has beat down cancer and his physicians really cannot explain how he did it so quickly. President Carter knows exactly why, *simple faith*! President Carter had faith in his team around him: physicians, nurses, caretakers, family, friends, and loved ones. Most importantly, his wife. He also had faith in his God to help guide him through his journey. Of course, he had faith in himself that he could overcome this. Simple faith in all aspects of his journey. Never wavering, never doubting and always a simple faith. Make sure you have faith in all aspects of your journey. That faith will be good medicine for you.

DAY 38

Our philosophy is that we care about people first.
—Mark Zuckerberg, 1984-present
Co-Founder of Facebook

Exactly!! This should be everyone's motto! Show compassion, caring, love, encouragement, and on and on. These are the type of people you need on your team. They will keep you on the right track. They will keep your spirits up. They will be there on the good days and the bad days. You cannot measure how much this will help you. So, make sure everyone on your team cares about people first, including yourself.

I worked the majority of my career for just two companies. One of these companies embraced this philosophy 100%. They understood that their greatest asset was its people, the employees. This was one of the main reasons this company was very successful and still is to this day. They get a very high return on investment from their employees. The other company I worked for never understood the importance of this philosophy, even after many, many conversations from me about it. Their employees seemed to be just a number that could be replaced easily. I wish I had all the money this company wasted on turnover. I would be a very rich man. Treat your team like family, with love and care, and they will go to battle with you day in and day out.

DAY 39

Don't look back. Something might be gaining on you.
—Satchel Paige, 1906-1982
American Professional Baseball Player

Never look back over your shoulder as you move forward on your journey. Keep your eyes looking forward with an eye on the prize at the end. What has passed, has passed. No need to look back there. It will just slow you down. What happens when you slow down? You give cancer time to catch up and possibly do more damage. Keep pushing forward! Keep following the plan the physicians laid out for you. You can make this journey without looking back!

DAY 40

Work hard for what you want, because it won't come to you without a fight. You have to be strong and courageous and know that you can do anything you put your mind to. If somebody puts you down or criticizes you, just keep on believing in yourself and turn it into something positive.
—Leah LaBelle, 1986-present
American Singer

Wouldn't it be great if you heard these words from your physician when he gives you the cancer diagnosis? You know this journey will be hard and filled with obstacles. This will be the most difficult challenge of your life. You must fight hard for it. Keep your mind focused on the fight. You can do anything you put your mind to. Don't let it become foggy with other things. Let your cancer know that you are completely focused on it and you are going to keep your eyes on it. Be the strong person you are. You will need all the courage you have stored up for this fight as well. Turn any negative thing you come across into something positive. We believe in you and so should you!

DAY 41

> *Your attitude is like a box of crayons that color your world. Constantly color your picture gray and your picture will always be bleak. Try adding some bright colors to the picture by including humor and your picture begins to brighten up.*
> —Allen Klein, 1931-2009
> American Businessman

Grab your box of crayons and dig through it. Take all the grays, blacks, and browns out and throw them away. You need *no* bleakness on this journey of yours. Keep the nice bright colors to use. Then you can keep this journey nice and bright. As you let humor in from your team, you will find more and more bright crayons in your box. Smiles and laughs are worth millions to you on this journey. The more you get, the brighter your path will be. You will be able to see and avoid all the potholes, mud puddles, sharp turns, steep hills, narrow bridges, and any detours that may pop up. Keep it bright, smile, and laugh. You will feel better and your attitude will be better!

DAY 42

There is no hope unmingled with fear, no fear unmingled with hope.
        —Baruch Spinoza, 1632-1677
        Dutch Philosopher

It is only natural to have fear because of your cancer. With that fear though, comes hope. Hope for a better tomorrow. Hope for a smooth journey with this cancer. Hope that this cancer will not spread within your body. Hope that you have a solid team around you to assist you on this journey. Hope that the plan your physicians laid out for you will work. Hope that you will remain strong throughout this journey. Hope that your faith will remain strong. Hope that your attitude stays positive throughout. Hope that you will many, many more tomorrows. Hope that one of those tomorrows will be cancer-free.

DAY 43

Let us sacrifice our today, so that our children can have a better tomorrow.
　　　　　—A.P.J. Abdul Kalam, 1931-2015
　　　　　　　　11th President of India

Let us sacrifice our today so that our cancer patient can have a better tomorrow. The team you assembled around you will be sacrificing their todays, so you can have a better tomorrow and many more of them. They will do it gladly for you as well. Just as you would do the same for them. They will give you their time, love, humor, and all those good things to keep moving down the road of your journey. This is a journey that cannot be made alone. Your team is very important. Keep them close. Their sacrifice for you is also for them. Nobody wants to lose you.

DAY 44

When you have a dream, you've got to grab it and never let go.
—Carol Burnett, 1933-present
American Actress

You have a dream, I'm sure, that comes back every night. That dream of walking out of your treatment center ringing that brass bell, signifying that you are now cancer-free. Hold onto that dream each night! Let it be fuel for your journey. Let it be your hope. Let it be your inspiration. Dream it each and every night. Remember it each and every morning. Hold onto it tight. Never let it go. Never let anyone take this dream away from you.

DAY 45

Whoever is happy will make others happy, too.
—Anne Frank, 1929-1945
German Jewish Diarist

Happiness for you is that good medicine. You need it daily. When you assembled your team, hopefully you have that one person that can always make you happy no matter the circumstances. That one person that turns a gloomy day bright. That one person that turns frowns into smiles. That one person that turns tears into laughter. That one person whose laugh can be heard for miles. That person's happiness will soak right into you, uplifting you on the worst of days. What you are going through is not happy of course, but nothing is stopping you from having happy moments along the way. For those happy moments will carry you from day to day.

DAY 46

I do not like cancer here or there; I do not like cancer anywhere.
—Cat in the Hat, 1957-present
American Cartoon Character

It is not very often I would agree with a cat, but today I do! So, there is your humor, happiness, and smile for the day!

DAY 47

Just because we cannot see clearly the end of the road, that is no reason for not setting out on the essential journey.
—John F. Kennedy, 1917-1963
35th President of the United States

The end of your road cannot be seen clearly, either. Your essential journey must be made. Your outcome is still unknown. You must move forward each day. Fighting the fight. Battling the evil beast. It maybe months or years before the end of the road can be seen clearly. You must have resolve to get to that point.

When President Kennedy started our nation out on the race to space, we could not see clearly the end of that road. As he said, "That is no reason for not setting out on the essential journey." His bold steps started us on a journey that still continues today. Deeper and deeper into space we send space probes. We have accomplished much along the way. Just as a journey with cancer, the journey into space has been very difficult and with sacrifice. We as a nation did not stop though. We continued to press ever forward, looking for that end of the road, which is still unknown today. Continue your journey with cancer just like our nation has with space. With great determination and resolve. Not allowing setbacks and bad days to stop you from making progress. You know the end of the road is there somewhere and it will come into focus someday.

DAY 48

I plead with you—never, ever give up on hope, never doubt, never tire, and never become discouraged. Be not afraid.
—Saint John Paul II, 1920-2005
Polish Pope of the Catholic Church

These are great words from the beloved Saint. Words that should be very meaningful for you. Do not lose your expectation and desire to beat down cancer. Let your flame of hope burn brightly every day. Never doubt yourself that you can do this. Your team has no doubt. They will be with you the whole time, making sure you do not tire and you do not become discouraged. Be not afraid, for we are with you!

DAY 49

It's lack of faith that makes people afraid of meeting challenges, and I believed in myself.
—Muhammad Ali, 1942-2016
American Professional Boxer

Have complete trust and confidence in yourself and that will give you the faith you need to complete this journey. For this journey is a great challenge that will not be easy and will not be quick. Your faith will be tested many times during this journey. Do not let your faith waiver. Keep it ever strong.

I am not sure if anyone has ever met challenges with such faith as Muhammad Ali. He had all the confidence in world in himself and trusted in himself to back that confidence up. His boxing career record will never be matched: 56 wins, only five loses, 37 knockouts, one Olympic Gold Medal, three-time Heavy Weight Champion of the World and had one span of his career where he was unbeaten for 35 years! If you can just have 50% of Ali's faith, you will beat cancer's butt from here to the moon. Don't lose the faith and confidence in that person you see every morning in the mirror. Trust in that person

DAY 50

Try to be a rainbow in someone's cloud.
     —Maya Angelou, 1928-2014
       American Poet

Let your team members be your rainbows on those cloudy and gloomy days that you will encounter on this journey. They will brighten your spirit and give you hope that your journey will end at the rainbow's end with a big pot of cancer-free gold. You will feel like the richest person in the world being cancer-free. Your work for this will be hard and long. You will have paid your price for that gold. On those cloudy stormy days, remember that there is a rainbow to follow. Let that rainbow brighten up your spirit and hope.

DAY 51

Vitality shows in not only the ability to persist, but the ability to start over.
—F. Scott Fitzgerald, 1896-1940
American Novelist

Stay strong and actively battle on against your cancer. Be very persistent in this battle. This battle will not be easy and may be a long battle, a very long battle. Your vitality over this time will be key for you. Keep pushing, keep fighting each day. Some days you may need to reset and start the battle again.

Julie had great vitality throughout her journey. The original plan was to amputate her leg because the tumor in her hip was large and intermixed with muscle and nerves. The physicians hoped that by taking the whole tumor, they could keep it from spreading. So, in June of 1981 the amputated her leg. She was very strong and brave and showed vitality of a champion. She was a champion too, our family's champion. All went as planned until

December of 1981. Julie found more lumps and sure enough the cancer was back. So, it was back to the drawing board and start over with a new plan. She was so strong accepting this and restarting her battle. She could be the poster person for vitality.

Work hard at the plan the physicians laid out for you. Do understand that things may change and you may have to hit the restart button.

DAY 52

Your ordinary acts of love and hope point to the extraordinary promise that every human life is of inestimable value.
—Desmond Tutu, 1931-present
South African Theologian

Yes, every human life is of inestimable, immeasurable, incalculable, unfathomable, indeterminable, and measureless value. No one person more than another. We are all equal in this value. That is why your team will shower acts of love upon you. That is why they will constantly give you hope. The hope that this journey will end well. You need to be acceptant of acts shown towards you. You need them. Take them like medicine, because they are medicine for you.

DAY 53

The Wright Brothers flew right through the smoke screen of impossibility.
—Charles Kettering, 1876-1958
American Inventor

The Wright Brothers had a dream. They believed in their dream. They worked very hard to make that dream reality. They never gave up on their hope, faith, and determination. People told them they couldn't make this dream real. They said the dream was impossible and nothing but a dream. Those people put up a smoke screen of impossibility. The Wright Brothers never let any of that negativity stop them. They remained positive and determined. Then they did the impossible: they flew through that smoke screen right into history. A man flew for the first time.

As the Wright Brothers had a dream, so do you. Your dream to be cancer-free someday. You need to believe in your dream. Work hard to make that dream reality. Do not give up on your hope, faith, and determination. You may think at times, when you hurt and have little strength, that your dream is impossible. Some around may say the same. Don't let that negativity soak into you. Brush it off and remain positive. Be determined to make your dream real. Follow your plan and let your team help you. You, too can break through that smoke screen of impossibility and bring your dream to life.

DAY 54

Happiness is a choice. You can choose to be happy. There's going to be stress in life, but it's your choice whether you let it affect you or not.
—Valerie Bertinelli, 1960-present
American Actress

Make happiness your choice during this stressful journey with cancer. Don't let stress slowly turn your attitude to the negative. A negative attitude and unhappiness is fuel for your cancer to grow more powerful than it already is. Lean on your team to keep your happiness at high levels. That in turn will keep your attitude very positive. It will be like a fresh coat of armor to keep your cancer from growing. Happiness is a choice, a choice you need to make to have a successful journey.

DAY 55

Courage is not the absence of fear, but rather the judgement that something else is more important than fear.
—Ambrose Redmoon, 1933-1996
American Author

Your fear is that cancer within you. What to you is more important than that fear? For you it is being able to say you are cancer-free. Wanting to be free of your cancer will give you all the courage you need to battle the evil beast. Let that fear build courage in you. That courage will give you strength you did not know you had. Wear your badge of courage proudly as you fight on!

DAY 56

For a time, sorrow takes up the whole landscape, but joy will come again.
—Martha Whitmore Hickman, 1925-2015
American Author

The feelings you had when you were given your diagnosis of sadness, unhappiness, grief, dejection, and gloom left you in sorrow. You cannot let that sorrow control your landscape for very long. You need to bring joy back into your life. What can make you joyful in times like this? Think of the joyful times you have had with family, friends, and loved ones. Let that be fuel to for you to battle hard against cancer, so you will continue to have those joyful times with those special people. Think of the joy you have on days like Christmas. Let that be fuel for you to battle hard, so you will continue to have those joyful days. Put the sorrow behind you and find ways to bring the joy back into your life.

DAY 57

Cancer is only going to be a chapter in my life and not the whole story.
—Joe Wasser, present
Cancer Survivor

Do not let cancer be your whole story. There is so much to do, so much to see, so many people to meet, and so many places to go. There are many chapters you can have in your story. Fill your book with many and make that chapter on cancer a very short chapter.

I think about Julie when writing this one. She did not let cancer be her whole story. She added several chapters after her diagnosis and leg amputation. Her trip to the west coast to see Los Angeles and the Pacific Ocean. The writing of her poem, which has been since published. Learning to ski with just her one leg. Her trip to the east coast to visit family and see the Atlantic Ocean.

Don't let your chapters stop with cancer. You can write many more. Make your last chapter have a happy ending.

DAY 58

What you do today can improve all your tomorrows.
—Ralph Marston, 1907-1967
American Professional Soccer Player

Make strides each day towards your goal. Take those as small victories. One after another with your hard work, determination, faith, hope, persistence, and courage will lead you to many improved tomorrows. Improved tomorrows for you will be very beneficial to that tomorrow you want at the end of this journey.

DAY 59

In order to succeed, we must first believe that we can.
—Nikos Kazantzakis, 1883-1957
Greek Writer

Believe in yourself. Believe in your physicians. Believe in your team you assembled. Believe in the plan that you and the physicians have laid out. Don't ever lose hope. Don't ever lose your faith. Keep your attitude positive. Allow your team to help you on those hard days when you feel like you can't push forward. We all believe in you and believe that you will succeed.

DAY 60

You can't cross the sea merely by standing and staring at the water.
—Rabindranath Tagore, 1861-1941
Bengali Poet

That sea represents your cancer. In order to be free of cancer, you must get across it. Doing nothing but staring at it won't make it happen. That is why you map out your journey across the sea with your physicians. You assembled yourself a winning team. Now you and your team must build a sturdy boat to cross those troubled waters. The boat must be able to withstand storms, rain, wind, and high waves. Pull up anchor and set off on your journey. Don't look back; stay focused on your plan. There will be days of calm seas and days of rough seas. Don't lose hope. Have complete faith that your journey will reach the other side of the sea where cancer does not exist.

DAY 61

You cannot have a positive life and a negative mind.
—Joyce Meyer, 1943-present
American Christian Author

You cannot have a positive outcome with your cancer and a negative mind. With a positive mind come positive results. Of course, staying positive during this whole journey will be hard. You will endure pain and suffering at some points. You need to stay resilient. Try to recover quickly from those difficult days and keep moving forward. Let all the negative vibes bounce off you. Only let the positive vibes enter your mindset. Stay positive, stay positive, stay positive!

DAY 62

We make a living by what we get, but we make a life by what we give.
—Winston Churchill, 1874-1965
British Prime Minister

You, of course, want to make a life or should we say continue your life for a long time. Be positive with everyone you encounter. Especially your team of physicians, caretakers, family, friends ,and loved ones. In turn, you will receive that positivity back from them. Show your love for them and in return they will shower you with love. Show them compassion and in return they will show you compassion. Doing this gives you a double-edged sword. You giving of yourself to your team and they in return are giving of themselves to give you strength to fight cancer. Advantage to you with the double-edged sword as your weapon.

DAY 63

Life is not easy for any of us. But what of that? We must have perseverance and above all, confidence in ourselves. We must believe that we are gifted for something and that this thing must be attained.
—Marie Curie, 1867-1934
Polish Physicist

Life, for sure, is not easy for you right now. Your journey is difficult and long. Have perseverance for this long and difficult journey. Be steadfast as you move ever forward. Let your steadfastness give you self-assurance and confidence that you will conquer this difficult journey. Each day your confidence level grows. Each day the journey gets a little better. You have all the gifts you need to complete this journey. You know you must attain this. The other option of death is not your goal. Keep the faith! Keep the hope! Keep pushing forward each day.

DAY 64

Transformation is a process, and as life happens, there are tons of ups and downs. It's a journey of discovery—there are moments on mountaintops and moments in deep valleys of despair.
—Rick Warren, 1954-present
American Christian Author

Your transformation back to a healthy and cancer-free you is a long process you are now encountering. During this process, you will discover the true you. You will find strength you did not know you had. Your self-confidence you grow. You will realize how important faith and hope are. You will have days that feel as though you are atop the highest mountain, feeling like you could conquer the world. The next day you may be in a deep, dark valley, feeling weakness and pain. Don't lose hope on those days. Know that the mountain top could be in reach tomorrow.

DAY 65

There are no constraints on the human mind, no walls around the human spirit, no barriers to our progress except those we ourselves erect.
—Ronald Reagan, 1911-2004
40th President of the United States

Do not put constraints, barriers and walls around you! You need to be free from all of them to make progress on your journey. Let your mind think clearly and positively about the task at hand. Do not let your human spirit be walled up from the cancer you battle. Let no barriers cancer tries to erect slow you down on this journey and impede your progress. You alone can keep these three demons of cancer at bay with a positive mind and a positive outlook for your journey.

DAY 66

I have seen what a laugh can do. It can transform almost unbearable tears into something bearable, even hopeful.
—Bob Hope, 1903-2003
American Comedian

Comedy and laughter are good for you during this time. Well, really, good at any time. Cancer has not taken your funny bone away. You can laugh all you want. You can laugh until it makes you cry. Just find time to laugh and enjoy. The days you just need to stay in bed and gather strength, find a good, old Bob Hope movie to watch. The comedy from that movie will make you laugh all afternoon. Building your strength right back up. Those tough days become bearable and give you more hope that your journey will be positive. Comedy + laughter = good medicine for you!

DAY 67

Don't watch the clock; do what it does. Keep going.
—Sam Levenson, 1911-1980
American Journalist

Every second, every minute, every hour, and every day are very important for you. You have no time to waste. Keep pushing forward. Anytime you stop or slow down, you are giving the evil beast a chance to catch up and do more damage. You don't need to look back over your shoulder, because the evil beast is still there, trying to catch you. Make progress each day. Even if it is just small progress, it is still progress. Keep going!

DAY 68

The human body experiences a power gravitational pull in the direction of hope. That is why the patient's hopes are the physician's secret weapon. They are the hidden ingredients in any prescription.
—Norman Cousins, 1915-1990
American Author

Hope for you is of the upmost importance. Hope is what fuels you for the journey. Never run out of it and never let it get low. Your visits to the physician are fuel stops for hope. Your visits from family and friends are fuel stops for hope. A day of prayer and reflection are fuel stops for hope. There will be plenty of opportunities for fuel stops on this journey. Don't miss any of those opportunities! For hope is the light of your soul, don't let it turn off!

DAY 69

Trust yourself. Create the kind of self that you will be happy to live with all your life. Make

the most of yourself by fanning the tiny, inner sparks of possibility into flames of achievement.
—Golda Meir, 1898-1978
4th Prime Minister of Israel

Don't let your cancer erode your trust in yourself. Your whole team has complete trust in you. So, do not lose that trust yourself! Let that trust grow stronger each day of your journey. As your trust grows stronger each day, it fans your inner sparks of possibility. Day after day of fanning and those sparks become flames that will engulf cancer and lead you to your greatest achievement: a you that is cancer-free!

DAY 70

Live your beliefs and you can turn the world around.
—Henry David Thoreau, 1817-1862
American Poet

Stick to your belief that you will overcome this setback with cancer. Live this belief each day. Think of this belief each morning you wake. Think of this belief each night you lay your head down to sleep. Never lose faith in this belief. Never lose hope in this belief. Never lose sight of this belief. Your strong belief will turn your world around and bring you back to the 100% healthy you.

DAY 71

Always make a total effort, even when odds are against you.
—Arnold Palmer, 1929-2016
American Professional Golfer

True in golf, true in life. The odds for you are not as great with your cancer. You still must make a total effort. Anything but a total effort could result in the loss of you. Arnold never had the odds in his favor. He did have his army, which you have yours. He did not have the true golfer's swing. He did have persistence, dedication, faith, and always gave a total effort. Because of that he was one of the greatest golfers of all time. He won seven major golf championships, he won 62 PGA Tour events, played on six Ryder Cup Teams, won the United State Amateur Championship in 1954 and is in the Golf Hall of Fame. All those accomplishments with some crazy-looking swing. That swing didn't account for those stats. His total effort in each tournament, on each hole, and with each swing accounted for those stats.

If Arnold could amass a career record like he did with his odds, you can kick cancer's butt with your odds and a complete total effort like Arnold's!

DAY 72

Out of difficulties grow miracles.
—Jean De La Bruyere, 1645-1696
French Philosopher

The cancer within you is a major difficulty. With your hard work, determination, faith, hope, persistence, courage, positive attitude, dedication, strong support team, and a little bit of love you can produce a miracle out of this difficulty. That miracle being your cure from the cancer.

DAY 73

The best portion of a good man's life, his little, nameless unremembered acts of kindness.
—William Wordsworth, 1770-1850
English Poet

Little acts of kindness showered upon you from your team could add up to bring you the best portion of your life. That would be your complete victory over cancer. For those acts of kindness showered on you keep you positive, grow your faith, give you more hope, fuel your determination, give you strength you didn't know you had, restore your confidence daily, and double up your courage. All of which gives you everything you need to complete your journey victorious! Let your support team know to keep on dispensing that good medicine: kindness.

DAY 74

Nothing can stop the man with the right mental attitude from achieving his goal; nothing on earth can help the man with the wrong mental attitude.
—Thomas Jefferson, 1743-1826
3rd President of the United States

You've heard it a thousand times from everyone—that a positive attitude is needed daily to complete your journey. Well, it is so very important! That right mental attitude gives you the fuel to fight off the evil beast, cancer. If you don't have it daily, the wrong mental attitude fuels the evil beast. When the evil beast continues to get fuel day after day, nothing on this earth will stop him. Your complete demise because of the lack of the right mental attitude will be met. Stay positive every day. Lean on your team to help keep you positive on those difficult days. Don't fuel the beast.

DAY 75

I learned that courage was not the absence of fear, but the triumph over it. The brave man is not he who does not feel afraid, but he who conquers that fear.
—Nelson Mandela, 1918-2013
President of South Africa

Mr. Mandela had more courage than that of a hundred men. He waged an anti-apartheid campaign for more than 20 years in South Africa. He was jailed for that fight. He spent 27 years in jail. He was one of eight men that were sentenced to life in prison for sabotage and conspiracy to overthrow the government. In 1989 South African President F.W. de Klerk put an end to apartheid. Several months later, de Klerk ordered the release of Mandela from prison. His 27 years in prison were brutal. He was forced to do hard labor. He had no bed in his cell or running water. He remained the leader of the anti-apartheid movement while in prison. In 1993, Mandela and de Klerk were awarded the Nobel Peace Prize for putting an end to apartheid in South Africa. One year later, Nelson Mandel became President of South Africa.

Be as brave as Mr. Mandela! Fear is very real for you right now. Just as Mandela conquered his fear and ended apartheid, so can you conquer your fear with cancer and triumph over it! We know you can do it!

DAY 76

Every great dream begins with a dreamer. Always remember, you have within you the strength, the patience, and the passion to reach for the stars to change the world.
—Harriet Tubman, 1822-1913
American Abolitionist

Create your dream of beating down cancer. Gather all your strength, patience and passion and dream away...

You are a knight on a beautiful white horse with the magical silver sword. Have patience for the evil beast to show his ugly face. Then let your great strength and passion to defeat him take over. Take your magical silver sword and pierce the heart of the evil beast. You've changed your world and become cancer-free!

Live your dream out!

DAY 77

Calm mind brings inner strength and self-confidence, so that's very important for good health.
　　　　　　—Dalai Lama, 1935-present
　　　　　　　　　　14th Dalai Lama

Stay calm throughout this battle with cancer. Remember you have a great team around you: physicians, nurses, caretakers, family, friends, loved ones, and people you don't even know. Let your inner strength and self-confidence grow to where nothing can defeat you. Find what calms your mind the best. Maybe it's going to the beach and sitting there listening to the waves. Maybe it's going to a park and sitting amongst the tress and listening to the wind whistle through the leaves. Maybe it's just laying at home listening to your favorite music. Find what works best for you and be calm!

DAY 78

The key is to keep company only with people who uplift you, whose presence calls forth your best.
　　　　　　—Epictetus, 50AD-135AD
　　　　　　　　　　Greek Philosopher

You need your best daily. Don't let negative people diminish your best. Surround yourself with positive and compassionate people. They will uplift you with their love and support for you, which will inspire you to give your best every day. Anything but your best daily gives cancer the opportunity to give its best, which could mean it may spread and grow stronger. You do not want that to happen. Keep the best possible team around you. You will be uplifted!

I remember Jim talking about this shortly after he started his journey. He always had a lot of people stopping in at his shop to talk with him and have a cup of coffee. He said he needed to cut some of that out. He said, "I only have so much time left. I don't need to sit and listen to some of those guys that always complain about this and that and are negative." He had several of those types that stopped in. Not only was he uplifted more by his close circle, he had more time to do what he needed to do to finish his list. Not his bucket list, but his "I want to do while I still can" list. Jim know exactly what Epictetus meant when he said it back 100AD or so.

DAY 79

Things do not happen. Things are made to happen.
—John F. Kennedy, 1917-1963
35th President of the United States

You were made to happen! Make things happen for you. Do not let cancer unmake you. It is your destiny to knock cancer out and ensure you for a very long time. Give it your best every day. Don't sit back and think that this will take care of itself with just the medicine and treatments from your physicians. Those are just two ingredients in a long list of what you need to knock cancer out. Do not wait till tomorrow to do what can be done today!

Make it happen!

DAY 80

Mental toughness is spartanism with qualities of sacrifice, self-denial, dedication. It is fearlessness and it is love.
—Vince Lombardi, 1913-1970
American Professional Football Coach

Vince Lombardi instilled this mental toughness into his players as a head coach in the National Football

League. This was part of his famous single-minded determination to win. His players bought into his program and allowed the Green Bay Packers to win five Championships under Vince. Vince's five Championships are the most by any one coach in the National Football League.

As you can see, mental toughness is a trait you must have for your journey with cancer. You will have to make sacrifices along the way but stay dedicated to a complete victory over cancer. Your team will be fearless as they love and defend you. Be the Spartan that defeats cancer.

DAY 81

There are no secrets to success. It is the result of preparation, hard work and learning from failure.
—Colin Powell, 1937-present
65th Sec. of State & U.S. Army General

Your physicians laid out the groundwork for your battle with cancer. Fully preparing them, you and your team. You need to make sure you understand that plan fully. Your team must understand it as well. The hard work falls upon your shoulders. You need to get up each day ready to battle the evil beast. Your team will be there for you on those hard days when you need some love and compassion to fuel your tired body and mind. Know that your physicians are working hard on their end, as well. Making sure your plan is working and that you are on the right path. You will have setbacks. Those setbacks are opportunities to learn from for you and your physicians. You may need to adjust your prepared plan to get by those setbacks. Do this and trust in this and you may see success!

DAY 82

Love is when the other person's happiness is more important than your own.
—H. Jackson Brown Jr., 1940-present
American Author

Your team members know your happiness is more important than theirs. Their love for you will bring you an abundance of happiness. Let that happiness fuel you to battle another hour, another day, another week, another month, another year...

In October 2015 all six of us brothers were able to get together for a whole week and spend time with Jim. Naturally, we showered him with love. This time we spent with Jim meant so much to him. You could see the happiness written upon his face all week. I strongly feel this week together gave Jim the fuel to live several more weeks. It also meant so much to each of us brothers.

Share your love and happiness with others. Accept love from others to increase your happiness. Make it a complete circle of love and happiness.

DAY 83

What's the worst thing that can happen to a quarterback? He loses his confidence.
—Terry Bradshaw, 1948-present
American Professional Football Player

What's the worst thing that can happen to a cancer patient? He loses his confidence. Well, it may not be the absolute worst thing that can happen, but it is near the top of the list. Don't ever lose confidence in yourself during this journey. Keep the trust that the plan for this journey will work. Keep the belief that you will remain strong enough to complete this journey. Keep the faith that your team with be right there with the whole time. Keep the conviction that this cancer is beatable. Keep the confidence!

DAY 84

Music has healing power. It has the ability to take people out of themselves for a few hours.
— Elton John, 1947-present
English singer-songwriter

When you're having a bad day, your strength is low, your pain is great, put your favorite music on. Lay down and close your eyes. Let the music take you away from your battle at hand, away from the weakness, and away from the pain. Let it heal you for this day.

When Jim was working at his shop during his journey and he started to get weak and felt the pain rising, he would go upstairs to his loft. He would turn on some of his favorite music and lay down on the couch. He let that music take him away for an hour or two. Away from the weakness, away from the pain, and mostly away from the damn cancer. When the music had done its trick, he would come back down to the shop reenergized ready to push on. Music does have some sort of healing power to it.

DAY 85

I've only had two rules: do all you can and do it the best you can. It's the only way you ever get that feeling of accomplishing something.
—Colonel Sanders, 1890-1980
Founder of Kentucky Fried Chicken

These are two good rules for you to follow on your journey. The rules worked very well for the Colonel. The Colonel's real name is Harland. He started to be called Colonel in 1935 when the governor of Kentucky designated him a true Kentucky colonel because his chicken was the best chicken in the world. The Colonel began to franchise his chicken in 1952. By 1964, he had more than 600 franchised outlets. He sold his rights that year for $2 million. So, yes, these two rules could serve you well.

Do all you can do each day. Put forth an effort every day, knowing that on those hard days, small success is still success and you did all you could do. Do it the best you can. Give your best effort each day. Give 100% of what you have on that day. Your 100% will change day to day because of that cancer.

My Uncle Abe always told me something very similar to Colonel Sanders's two rules. He said, "Doing a job large or small, do it right or not at all!"

Makes these your personal rules for your journey with cancer.

DAY 86

Obstacles don't have to stop you. If you run into a wall, don't turn around and give up. Figure out how to climb it, go through it, or work around it.
—Michael Jordan, 1963—present
American Professional Basketball Player

You've run into a wall in your life: cancer. It is just an obstacle. Don't let it stop you. Don't turn around and give up. You and your team have a solid plan to climb over it, go through it or work around it. Obstacles are meant to be overcome. It is just a small hinderance along the way. This wall will seem smaller and smaller as long as you keep your positive attitude, courage, determination, faith, hope, and persistence. You can do it! Or as Michael would say, "Just do it!"

DAY 87

The riskiest thing we can do is maintain the status quo.
—Bob Iger, 1951-present
CEO/COB of Walt Disney Co.

Maintaining the status quo for you is very risky! For you, the status quo cannot be an option. If it is, you are giving cancer every opportunity possible to continue to wreak havoc on your body. Spreading to more places and more than likely taking you down for the count. So, work your plan and let your team support you. Be aggressive and relentless in your battle with cancer. The status quo is for lazy people that think they are comfortable. You're not lazy and with cancer, we darn well know you're not comfortable!

DAY 88

Happiness radiates like the fragrance from a flower and draws all good things towards you.
—Maharishi Mahesh Yogi, 1918-2008
Spiritual Leader

Find some happiness daily. Let that happiness draw strength, confidence, endurance, and determination unto you. These are medications you must have daily to keeping pressing forward on your journey. Happiness can bring you much of what you need to be successful on this journey. Find your happiness!

DAY 89

Cancer has given me a dose of humility. I'm much more empathetic. It's a club I would rather not have joined, but it is a club.
—Tom Brokaw, 1940-present
American News Journalist

I'm sure you felt something like Mr. Brokaw. You were cruising along in your life, feeling good and untouchable until you received that cancer diagnosis. It gave you a pretty large dose of humility. You were humbled and maybe felt a bit meek. Rightfully so, when slapped in the face with cancer. That would take the wheels out from under the best of us. If there is a silver lining to those storm clouds, it is that you will be much more empathetic. You will be able to understand and share the feelings of others in the same boat as you. Like Mr. Brokaw said, "it's a club." You now have charter membership to this club. Use this club as a resource and brotherhood. Share your thoughts and feelings with the other members. You may pick up on things that could benefit you. Also share your frustrations with them. They may have experienced the same and have solutions. Welcome to the club!

DAY 90

My success just evolved from working hard at the business at hand each day.
—Johnny Carson, 1925-2005
American Comedian

Johnny did work hard at the business at hand each day. He started in broadcasting in 1950 in Omaha. In twelve short years he made it to be the host of *The Tonight Show* on NBC. He hosted that show for 30 years, becoming an American icon. He won six Emmy Awards, Television Academy's Governor's Award, Peabody Award, Television Academy Hall of Fame, Presidential Medal of Freedom, and a Kennedy Center Honor. He was born in Corning, Iowa and used his good Iowa work ethic to reach great heights in television. The business at hand for you is putting cancer out to pasture. You need to work hard each day on your team's plan for your journey with cancer. Try to have a small success each day. Keep building on those throughout the journey and let them lead you to that big success you desire. Don't be distracted from the business at hand. Don't put off today's business at hand until tomorrow. Don't blow it off because something more fun popped up to do. Don't skip it because you don't feel up to it today. Like Johnny said, work hard at the business at hand each day!

DAY 91

Don't worry about your heart; it will last you as long as you live.
—W.C. Fields, 1880-1946
American Comedian

Thank you, Captain Obvious, W.C. Fields. In truth though, don't worry about your heart, about your stubbed toe or your runny nose. All of your attention needs to be directed towards the cancer. You need every fiber of your being to battle cancer. Don't let anything distract from that battle. Focus, focus, focus.

DAY 92

It's not who I am underneath, but what I do that defines me.
—Batman, 1939-present
American Fictional Superhero

What will you do to define yourself? I will give you a total of three guesses and the first two do not count. That's right, you're going to battle the evil beast with all the might of Batman. Give it to the evil beast just like he would with some *pow, crash, bang, boom, zap, bam, zoom, bonk, clank, crunch, plop, sock, splat, slosh, zam, kapow, clunk* and last, but not least, a big, old *biff!* Then your Robin, physician, would say, "Holy smokes, Batman—I think you did it!" You put down the evil beast and defined yourself clearly as a true superhero!

DAY 93

Weakness of attitude becomes weakness of character.
    —Albert Einstein, 1879-1955
    German Theoretical Physicist

Don't let your cancer eat away at you and weaken your attitude. Let your attitude remain strong and positive, building your character each day during this journey. You have read it here several times to keep a positive attitude. Yes, it is hard under your circumstances, but so very important to do so. Your strong positive attitude will help you keep a positive outlook on your journey, will give you a positive perspective on the situation and will let you approach this whole journey positively. Negativity will breed more negativity, which will lead to a negative outcome. Don't let your attitude weaken! Keep you character strong!

DAY 94

When you're trying to accomplish lofty goals, and when you're attacking something of great magnitude, you have to have help.
—Zach Johnson, 1976-present
American Professional Golfer

You have a lofty goal and you are attacking something of great magnitude. You will need help along the way. That help is your team we have spoken about throughout this book. Let yourself be open to those team members. They are there to help you, support you, empower you, and inform you. Cancer patients with a strong emotional support team adjust better to the changes cancer brings to their lives. Your outlook will be more positive, giving you a better quality of life through this journey.

Zach did not win the Master's Tournament and the British Open by himself. Golfers, like you, battle on the front lines alone. But, they have a team behind them, just like you have or should have. The Masters and the British Open are two of golf's biggest prizes. Zach had a great team to support him in both those victories. You should have a great team to support you and have a victory of great magnitude like Zach Johnson did.

DAY 95

In this situation I was constantly exposed to danger and death.
—Daniel Boone, 1734-1820
American Pioneer

Just as Daniel Boone was constantly exposed to danger and death in the Kentucky Hills, you will endure the same on your journey with cancer. Daniel had several dangerous run-ins with Native Americans in his time. You need to be ready to have some dangerous run-ins with your cancer during your journey. Daniel's daughter was once kidnapped by Native Americans. Good old Daniel went right out there and rescued her. He, himself was kidnapped by the Native Americans. Daniel, being the fighter he was, escaped from them. He was also captured once and released. Told never to return. Daniel overcame all those dangerous situations and became famous from them. You can overcome any obstacles you come across on your journey, as well. You then will be famous to us for beating cancer. So, get your beaver hat and rifle, just like Daniel, and complete your journey.

DAY 96

Where there is no vision, there is no hope.
       —George Washington Carver, 1864-1943
                American Inventor

Keep your vision clear throughout your journey. Do that by keeping your attitude positive, your faith strong, your determination relentless, your courage plenty, and your team close. Without that clear vision, you will crash and burn, giving you no hope!

Where would we be today without George Washington Carver's vision? If you want to be amazed, Google all of his inventions. The list goes on and on. Over 300 just with peanuts and over 500 different shades of dye. His work was monumental to the agriculture industry here in the United States. He made this world a better place to live in because of his vision.

What will your vision do for you?

DAY 97

It is often when night looks darkest, it is often before the fever breaks that one senses the gathering momentum for change, when one feels that resurrection of hope in the midst of despair and apathy.
           —Hillary Clinton, 1947-present
        First Lady of the U.S. & U.S. Senator

Hopefully you feel that resurrection of hope each time your night is at its darkest and your fever is about to break. You will have feelings of despair and apathy during your journey. Remember, hope is just right around the corner from those two. When despair and apathy try to get into your head, turn to your team to pull you through and around the corner to hope!

DAY 98

I will seize fate by the throat; it shall certainly never wholly overcome me.
    —Ludwig van Beethoven, 1770-1827
        German Composer

Seize the fate of your cancer by the throat and do not allow it to overcome you! Is it kismet for you? Possible. Is it fortune for you? Maybe. Is it your destiny? Why, yes, it is! This is your destiny!

DAY 99

Peace is a journey of a thousand miles and it must be taken one step at a time.
    —Lyndon B. Johnson, 1908-1973
    36th President of the United States

Cancer is a journey of a thousand miles and it must be taken one step at a time. Cancer is very similar to peace. It takes a long time to overcome it. It is very hard to get both sides to agree on a settlement. Cancer does not want to negotiate with anyone at any time. Pretty much the same as the communists of Vietnam. Cancer will put up a very tough fight, just as the communists did in Vietnam. It may seem like your battle with cancer will never end. Just as the American people felt about the war in Vietnam. You must, as the President said, take one step at a time. Don't lose hope; keep pushing one step at a time all of the thousand miles!

DAY 100

I am determined to be cheerful and happy in whatever situation I may find myself. For I have learned that the greater part of our misery or unhappiness is determined not by our circumstances, but by our disposition.
 —Martha Washington, 1731-1802
Former 1st First Lady of the United States

Be determined, like Martha Washington was, to be cheerful and happy in the situation you find yourself in. The situation of battling cancer. No, cancer is not cheerful and happy. If the greater part of this misery of cancer can be controlled by your disposition, you would want to try to be as cheerful and happy as you can. Cheerfulness and happiness are both good medicine that your body, mind, and soul need during this battle. Some days you may not feel any of that; understandable. On the good days, get a little extra and put it in your bank!

DAY 101

However difficult life may seem, there is always something you can do and succeed at.
—Stephen Hawking, 1942-2018
English Theoretical Physicist

Mr. Hawking endured many difficulties in his life. He was very successful despite having ALS. He did not let ALS stop him or slow him down. He found a way to overcome what was thrown at him. In fact, the disease helped him become the noted scientist we remember today. When he was diagnosed at the age of 21, he didn't always focus on his studies. He said he was bored with life and there was really nothing to do. With the realization that he might not live long, he poured himself into his work and research. He went on to write or co-write 15 books and continued his research to the end of his life.

You can succeed through your difficulty of cancer. Your success would be to knock cancer out. With your determination, with the guidance of your physicians, with the support of your team, and with all your faith and hope you can do it! You have a lot of people to support you.

DAY 102

You just get up each day and put one foot in front of the other and go. You know each day is different.
—Nancy Reagan, 1921-2016
Former First Lady of the United States

When the going gets tough for you on this journey, you do just that. Get up each day and put one foot in front of the other and go. Go straight ahead on that path the physicians laid out for you. Don't look back, just ahead. This is a long journey and will take time. Some days you will make little progress. That is okay. On the days you're feeling better, you will make more progress. Each day will be different for you. Take what you can when you can.

DAY 103

You miss 100% of the shots you don't take.
   —Wayne Gretzky, 1961-present
   Canadian Professional Hockey Player

Wayne always took the shot when he had the opportunity. Because of that, he is known as the greatest hockey player of all time. He holds 40 regular season records. The grandest being most goals scored, 894. He also has 65 hat tricks in his career! Very evident that Wayne took a lot of shots.

Don't go down without taking shots at cancer. You can make some of those shots count and beat that evil beast! Keep your eye on the goal and fire away at it!

DAY 104

You always have something to learn from people who have been through more than you. Be open and receptive to what they know.
   —Zac Efron, 1987-present
   American Actor

Find a great mentor for yourself. A friend or someone you know that has been through the battle with cancer. Learn from their personal battle, what they did, and how they beat the beast. Their knowledge could give you the inside track to victory. Many, many successful people have had mentors they credit for their success. Here are just a few.

Socrates to Plato	Plato to Aristotle
Aristotle to Alexander the Great	Dr. Martin Luther King to Jesse Jackson
Mahatma Gandhi to Nelson Mandela	Ralph Waldo Emerson to Henry David Thoreau
George Mason to Thomas Jefferson	Audrey Hepburn to Elizabeth Taylor
Barbara Walters to Oprah Winfrey	Bing Crosby to Frank Sinatra
Warren Buffet to Bill Gates	Obi-Wan Kenobi to Luke Skywalker
Professor Dumbledore to Harry Potter	Stephen Spielberg to J.J. Abrams

DAY 105

Blues is a tonic for whatever ails you. I could play the blues and then not be blue anymore.
—B.B. King, 1925-2015
American Singer-Songwriter

When you have those cloudy, gloomy days where your cancer is giving you the blues, bring up some B.B. King music like *Let the Good Times Roll, Sweet Little Angel* or *To Know You is to Love You*. Listen away and watch your blues go away and give you the upper hand again.

DAY 106

We need more kindness, more compassion, more joy, more laughter. I definitely want to contribute to that.
—Ellen De Generes, 1958-present
American Comedian

Ellen has hit the nail on the head! We need this for everyone in the world. Just think what more kindness, compassion, joy, and laughter could do for cancer patients. Hopefully the team you assembled overflows with all of these and fills you full of them. All much needed for you during your journey. If you run low on joy and laughter, just tune into Ellen's show!

DAY 107

If you don't know where you are going, every road will get you nowhere.
—Henry Kissinger, 1923-present
American Diplomat

Make sure you have a complete understanding of where you are going with the plan your physicians laid out for you. You best know, so you head down the right road. Not knowing and going down a road to nowhere may lead you to the place nobody wants to go to. Ask a lot of questions and don't assume anything.

DAY 108

Good company in a journey makes the way seem shorter.
—Izaak Walton, 1593-1683
English Writer

I remember as a young boy going on vacation to St. Louis from Dubuque. Back then the trip was over six hours. That, my friends, is a long time for an 8-year-old going to the city of his favorite baseball team and Six Flags Amusement Park! Mom came up with several car games for all of us to play along the way: count semis, find all 50 state license plates, and find all the letters to the alphabet. We all played together as a family and had a great time and the next thing I knew, I could see the famous Arch. Good company, good times and good games made the trip seem very short.

Good conversation, good laughs, good times, and good, positive sharing with good company makes your journey with cancer seem shorter. Again, that is why I talk about your team so often in this book. It will mean so much to you to have a team that can do this for you and with you.

DAY 109

To feel brave, act as if you were brave; use all of your will to that end and a courage fit will very likely replace the fit of fear.
—William James, 1842-1910
American Philosopher

That fit of fear you have from the shock of finding out your cancer diagnosis can be overcome. Jim and Julie acted so brave in the face of their cancer. They used all of their will to be brave throughout their journey, which gave them the courage needed to continue day after day. A courage that would also ease their fear of death. They both faced their eventual deaths with courage and bravery. By their time, there was no fear. Their courage and bravery made their deaths easier for our family to accept.

DAY 110

Everybody needs beauty as well as bread, places to play in and pray in, where nature may heal and give strength to body and soul.
　　　　　　　　—John Muir, 1838-1914
　　　　　　　　Scottish—American Author

John Muir wrote this in 1912 and was referring to Yosemite in California. Yosemite had such great beauty that he believed it could heal and give strength to one's body and soul. Find that place for you. The place where you can go and be alone with nature. Let it soak into you, making you feel better and giving your body and soul strength. I am sure you know that spot as you read this. Go there, go there often to give your body and soul a spa day.

Julie had her special place in nature to go to. It was on the bluffs above the Mississippi River by the historical Eagle Point Park. The picture that graces the cover of this book is a picture of her at this spot. It meant so much to her that she had us scatter some of her ashes over that bluff, making it a special spot in nature for all of my family.

DAY 111

A man can succeed at almost anything for which he has unlimited enthusiasm.
—Charles Schwab, 1939-present
American Investor & Financial Executive

Build yourself up with great enthusiasm to wipe cancer out of your system. That positive thought process will be a deadly weapon to use on the evil beast, cancer. Keep the flames of your enthusiasm burning throughout your journey. Let your positive attitude, faith, hope, courage, and determination by the fuel for those flames.

DAY 112

All of us know someone who has been through difficult emotional times and we know how hard it can be to see a way forward.
—Kate Middleton, 1982-present
Duchess of Cambridge

You are going through difficult emotional times. At times your way forward may seem dark and foggy, with no light at the end of the tunnel. Lean on your team to help lift your emotions up. You can keep your emotions up with a daily diet of humor, laughter, time shared, and some of your favorite music. Times can be tough during this journey. Don't forget to keep some humor and laughter in it.

DAY 113

Most of us have far more courage than we ever dreamed we possessed.
　　　　　　　　—Dale Carnegie, 1888-1955
　　　　　　　　American Writer & Lecturer

You probably didn't know you had so much courage until you found out you have cancer. Your darkest moments often bring out the best in you. Let the courage you summoned push aside your fear, so you can battle that cancer each and every day!

DAY 114

The truest wisdom is a resolute determination.
　　　　　　　—Napoleon Bonaparte, 1808-1873
　　　　　　　French Emperor & Military Leader

Have a resolute determination like that of Napoleon. Napoleon's determination helped him to become one of the greatest military leaders of all time. In many of his battles, Napoleon's forces were outnumbered by his enemy. He never gave up and always had a plan of attack. He was determined to win all of his battles. Be determined to win all of your battles with cancer. If you don't win that final battle, you at least know you gave it your best and never gave up. You will go down as a hero.

DAY 115

Give light and the darkness will disappear of itself.
—Desiderius Erasmus, 1466-1536
Dutch Theologian

Keep the light switch on! How do you do that? Let your team do their work of keeping you uplifted throughout your journey. They will shed light upon you with their love, compassion, and care for you. You help keep that light on by maintaining a positive attitude, wearing your badge of courage, and keeping your faith. Don't let the evil beast make the room dark! Let the light shine on!

DAY 116

Problems are not stop signs, they are guidelines.
—Robert H. Schuller, 1926-2015
American Christian Televangelist

Don't stop your journey because of a small problem. Keep pushing forward on that journey. Don't let anything slow you down. If the cancer police pull you over for running the stop sign and give you a ticket, rip it up and hand it back. Tell the cancer police you don't have time for that or time for them. Then get back on the accelerator and down the road of your journey.

DAY 117

The purpose of human life is to serve and show compassion and the will to help others.
—Albert Schweitzer, 1875-1965
French-German Theologian

We are called to serve the moment we are born. We are not here for ourselves. The team you have around you understands that and are willing to give of themselves to help you. Showing you compassion and love should come easy for them. Little effort needed on their part to do that. As has been mentioned several times, that compassion and love they shower you with is important medicine for you. Take it in and take it in daily. Physician's orders!

DAY 118

Life is a journey that must be traveled no matter how bad the roads and accommodations.
—Oliver Goldsmith, 1728-1774
Irish Novelist

The road you are on for your journey is a bit narrow and full of potholes, but just keep pushing down that road. The journey won't be easy at all. This narrow road with all its potholes will eventually lead you to a nice, wide, and smooth road. This super road leads right to a five-star hotel where the accommodations are all that you dreamed of.

Your journey must be traveled through those bad, narrow roads. Those tough days of travel will seem never ending, but they will lead you to better roads and the best accommodations. Keep pushing, keep your tank full, and keep a couple of spare tires with you. You can do it!

DAY 119

Where there is great love, there are always miracles.
—Willa Cather, 1873-1947
American Author

Let love produce a miracle for you. Let it help you eject the cancer from within. Share, in great abundance, your love for your family, friends, and your team. In return, they will bring their love unto you. A good person is not afraid to say, "I love you!" Let all that love create a circle of love around your team and produce a miracle.

DAY 120

Let your heart feel for the afflictions and distress of everyone and let your hand give in proportion to your purse.
 —George Washington, 1732-1799
 1st President of the United States

All good hearts should feel for the afflictions and distress of a cancer patient. The team around has shown their good heart by coming to your side for this journey of yours. The hope is that all the people you know should feel also. If their hand cannot give of their purse, may they give of themselves some love, happiness, compassion, and time, which brings you strength that you need. If their purse runneth over, may they donate to a worthy cancer foundation like the Avery Foundation.

DAY 121

Life is a journey. When we stop, things don't go right.
—Pope Francis, 1936-present
Argentine Pope of the Catholic Church

You are in the midst of your journey with cancer. Do not stop! Keep pushing forward. Don't give your cancer a chance to catch up and do more damage. Do not stop! Keep pushing forward. Wake up each day and tell yourself that you will make some progress, even if it is just a little. Each day you make progress is a victory for you. Don't let things go bad!

DAY 122

Strength and growth come only through continuous effort and struggle.
—Napoleon Hill, 1883-1970
American Author

Don't let up! Keep giving a continuous effort to beat cancer. Yes, it is a struggle, but you have great strength. Far more than you think you have. Your efforts today give you strength for tomorrow. Your effort plus strength equals growth towards your ultimate goal of beating this cancer.

DAY 123

You build on failure. You use it as a stepping stone. Close the door on the past. You don't try to forget the mistakes, but don't dwell on it. You don't let it have any of your energy, or any of your time, or any of your space.
—Johnny Cash 1932—2003
American Singer-Songwriter

Don't let the failure of a bad day eat at your confidence. Just look to Johnny's career as a perfect example of this. He reached over 90 million records sold before his death. He would never have reached that level if he didn't build off his failures. Not all his songs he wrote and sang were hits or even made it to albums. He kept working and producing hits, learning from failed songs. You will need to do the same. Use it as energy for the tomorrow, a stepping stone to future gains on your cancer. Every day won't be a victory. When it's a bad day, close the door on it and don't dwell on it. When you dwell on it, you let it take energy from you, time from you and space. You cannot afford to give any of that up. Keep your chin up and keep on keeping on.

DAY 124

Let your hopes, not your hurts, shape your future.
—Robert H. Schuller, 1926-2015
American Christian Televangelist

You will have hurts, there is no avoiding that. Do not let those hurts dictate your future by eroding your hopes. Your future depends on your hope. That hope of beating your cancer. Don't lose this desire to beat it. You have help; use it.

Jim had a hope for himself to complete his "chemo bike" invention before he became too sick to or passed away. He worked so very hard to do this. Working some days when he should not have because he was in such pain from his cancer. He did not let that hurt stop him. His hope, his desire was to get that bike done. Nothing was going to stop him from fulfilling that hope and making it reality. And he did just that. He completed that invention. That invention along with his international award-winning Avery Dicycle were donated to the City of Dubuque to be displayed at a suitable location. Sharing a bit of his legacy with his community.

DAY 125

Your bat is your life. It's your weapon. You don't want to go into battle with anything that feels less than perfect.
—Lou Brock, 1939-present
American Professional Baseball Player

Lou took his bat to work with him every day as a player for the St. Louis Cardinals. He used that bat for 3023 career hits, a .293 career batting average, eight years hitting over .300, six All Star selections, a post-season average of .391, and a selection into baseball's Hall of Fame. A bat well used, I would say.

For you, your faith is your life. It's your bat, your weapon to use against cancer. Make sure your faith is strong and not damaged by your cancer. You need it to be perfect for the battle you are in. It needs to feel good, like your favorite t-shirt. Your faith nurtures all the other weapons you will need for your battle, hope, desire, determination, positive attitude, love, strength, and happiness.

DAY 126

You simply have to put one foot in front of the other and keep going. Put blinders on and plow right ahead.
—George Lucas, 1944-present
American Filmmaker

You have heard similar quotes like this already. If you're like me, it is good to be reminded of such important things. This is just how you need to handle your journey, one foot in front of the other in front of the other in front of the other again, again, and again. Just keep going and going. Don't let anything distract you along the way. Keep your blinders on and don't look back.

DAY 127

I can't imagine a person becoming a success who doesn't give this game of life everything he's got.
—Walter Cronkite, 1916-2009
American News Journalist

Be a success by giving this battle everything you got. Get up each day with the positive attitude that you can do this. Try to make progress each day. Give it everything you got. Some days that everything is a little, but that is okay!

Julie gave it her all every day. Even through the days of heavy chemotherapy. She would get real sick after those treatments, but still would give it her everything. Each day was a battle and she fought it. She accomplished many things during her battle. She was a huge success even though she lost the battle to cancer. She is still a success today by the legacy she left us all.

DAY 128

Every time you find some humor in a difficult situation, you win.

—Sue Fitzmaurice
New Zealand Author

You, of course, are in a difficult situation with your battle against cancer. Humor is great medicine for you. It will give you a jolt of energy and strength. It would be like drinking a few cans of Red Bull. Try and take a dose of humor each day. You want some humor? Watch some Rodney Dangerfield, Tim Conway, Robin Williams, *Seinfeld*, *The Big Bang*, *Caddyshack*, *Animal House*, *Fast Times at Ridgemont High*, *Mrs. Doubtfire* or *Grumpy Old Men*.

Those are just a few that would bring me a lot of humor and laughter.

What's the easiest way to remember your wife's birthday? Forget it once. What do smart blondes and UFOs have in common? You always hear about them, but you never see them.

DAY 129

Courage is contagious. When a brave man takes a stand, the spines of others are often stiffened.
—Billy Graham, 1918-present
American Christian Evangelist

You have been brave, you have taken a stand against the cancer that has taken up residency within you. That courage to do so will rub off on your team and stiffen their spines to be able to support you even more so than before. No one should ever say that you are not brave. Facing down cancer is one of the bravest things that I can think of. Facing down cancer is looking the Grim Reaper in the face and saying, "Not today, buddy!"

DAY 130

I dwell in possibility.
—Emily Dickinson, 1830-1886
American Poet

You should also dwell in possibility. The possibility that things will get better. The possibility that your journey with cancer will be short. The possibility that you will not suffer much pain. The possibility that your determination will not weaken. The possibility that your faith remains strong. The possibility that hope will shine bright. The possibility that compassion and love will be showered upon you. The possibility that your strength carries you through. The possibility that the light at the end of the tunnel gets bigger and bigger each day. The possibility that you will beat this cancer. The possibility that you will have a long, full life. The possibility that one day we will have a cure for this evil beast!

DAY 131

Our attitudes control our lives. Attitudes are a secret power working 24 hours a day, for good or bad. It is of paramount importance that we know how to harness and control this great force.
—Irving Berlin, 1888-1989
American Composer

Your attitude could make all the difference in world in how your journey ends up. Your attitude never stops working for you or against you. You are the one who decides if it helps you or fights you. How you handle each moment of the day is dictated by your attitude. It is of paramount importance for you during this journey that you maintain a positive attitude. You do not need anything else working against you. Cancer is more than one can handle already. Having a negative attitude gives cancer a stealth bomber that can deliver more cancer bombs throughout your body. It is hard, but please harness your attitude. Keep it in check as positive. May this force be with you!

DAY 132

We are going as fast as we can as soon as we can. We're in a race against time.
—Jack Nicholson, 1937-present
American Actor

You too, are in a race against time. Your time is very valuable because of the cancer you have. You need to make use of each minute. You do not want to give the cancer any time at all. Giving it time is breathing more life into it. Giving it the opportunity to grow. Go as fast as you can, as soon as you can down the path of your journey. Don't look back. Don't get distracted. Don't take any "shortcuts". Stay on the mapped-out route from your doctors. Don't stop until you reach your destination!

DAY 133

It doesn't take a hero to order men into battle. It takes a hero to be one of those men who goes into battle.
—Norman Schwarzkopf, 1934-2012
American Army General

Your physician that has given you your marching orders into the battle against cancer is not the hero. You are the hero for taking those orders and marching off to war. For this war is just as scary as any war—WWI, WWII, Korean, Vietnam, and Gulf War—because it has death looming over it as well.

General Schwarzkopf never took credit for the victories in the Gulf War. He always gave that to his troops. He always pointed out that they were the heroes. They were on the front lines facing the enemy, not him. I'm sure your physicians are the same as the General. They will let all know that you are the hero. You are the one on the front line facing cancer. Keep battling! You are our hero!

DAY 134

Our goals can only be reached through a vehicle of a plan, in which we must fervently believe, and upon which we must vigorously act. There is no other route to success.
—Pablo Picasso, 1881-1973
Spanish Artist

This is very true for your goal of beating cancer. Your plan, road map for your journey, that the physicians laid out for you is what you must wholly believe in with passion. That is what can lead you to the Promised Land of good health, where cancer does not exist. To get there, you must work hard through some pain and suffering. It won't come easy. Your determination to get there with your hard work will lead to success. You fervently believed and vigorously battled; that is success. That is the route.

DAY 135

Laughter gives us distance. It allows us to step back from an event, deal with it and then move on.
—Bob Newhart, 1929-present
American Comedian

Ah yes, laughter is the best medicine. Let your laughter give you enough medicine to deal with your cancer and then move on to a more enjoyable life. With no worries about your health. No worries about all the medical bills. No worries about what appointments and where. Keep laughter in your daily plans. I know the couple episodes of Bob Newhart on *Big Bang Theory* make me laugh a lot. Try that.

DAY 136

I don't give up. I'm a plodder. People come and go, but I stay the course.
—Kevin Costner, 1955-present
American Actor

Don't give up, stay the course—have you heard that yet in this book? It is so true. You just have to keep pushing on. The great burden you carry on your shoulders for this journey may cause you to be a plodder at times. That burden of cancer is like carrying a ton of bricks on your back, which can make you feel like your feet are sinking in mud and you can barely drudge along. As Kevin said, just stay the course and don't give up!

DAY 137

I'll always use the negativity as more motivation to work even harder and become even stronger.
                    —Tim Tebow, 1987-present
                    American NFL & MLB Player

Use the negativity of cancer as your motivation to work hard each day and become even stronger to battle this evil beast. You will need more and more strength as you battle. It's a long battle that you will need to stay motivated for. If you get a bad report from a check-up, use it motivation. If you hear someone say you don't look good from the cancer, use it as motivation.

Tim Tebow constantly heard negative remarks about him while he was playing sports. While playing football for the University of Florida, he would drop to one knee and say a small prayer after making a touchdown or great play. Tim's parents were Baptist missionaries and he is still a devoted Christian. Many people said he should not be bringing his religion into the game. He just used that as motivation to do more, to be stronger. Well, Tim went on to become one of the greatest college football players in history. Listen to this list of awards: the Sullivan Award, the Davey O'Brien Award, the Maxwell Award, the Werfel Trophy, the Chic Harley Award, the Wooden Cup, the Manning Award, the Campbell Trophy, Touchdown Club of Columbus Quarterback of the Year Award, the AP College Football Player of the Year, the SEC Male Athlete of the Year, and the Heisman Trophy. He also led the Florida Gators to two BCS National Championships. You would think the negativity would stop right? It did not. Many people said he would not make it as an NFL player. He was drafted by the Denver Broncos and in 2011 led that team to the playoffs. Since he walked away from football, he is trying to make his way in professional baseball in the New York Mets organization. As you can imagine, he is hearing a lot of negativity again. It will be fun to see how baseball works out for him. I would never bet against Mr. Tebow. He has such determination and faith, I'm not sure there is anything he cannot do.

If you show a 1/10th of what Tebow did, you will kick cancer's butt! Be motivated! Be strong!

DAY 138

If you're going through hell, keep going.
— Winston Churchill, 1874-1965
British Prime Minister

You're in hell right now, battling cancer. Don't stop, keep pushing through. Pretty simple—hell just isn't a good place to be in. Number one, it is hot as heck there. You could sweat out all your bodily fluids. Number two, there are a lot of bad people that live there. Especially that devil guy! You could get hurt, stabbed, or robbed. Number three, everything is on fire there. You could get burnt pretty badly. Number four, it is underground. I don't know about you, but I like to stay above ground as long as possible! Four good reasons to keep going!

DAY 139

Everyone has inside of him a piece of good news. The good news is that you don't know how great you can be! How much you can love!

What you can accomplish! And what your potential is!
—Anne Frank, 1929-1945
German-Jewish Diarist

These words have even more power knowing who they came from and the conditions in which she lived under when writing them. Such a beautiful and positive attitude, considering. This was one strong teenager. You have a piece of good news inside of you as well. You don't know how great you can be, will be, and are. You don't know how much love you have. You don't know what you can accomplish and what your full potential is. Add that all up and you have a few more weapons than you thought to battle cancer.

If a young lady in hiding from the Nazis during World War II in Amsterdam believes in the good news inside everyone, you should surely believe in this and use it to your advantage. You have the potential to accomplish a cancer-free you!

DAY 140

If you see ten troubles coming down the road, you can be sure that nine will run into the ditch before they reach you.
—Calvin Coolidge, 1872-1933
30th President of the United States

You will come across troubles on your journey. Some will not make it to you and fall away. You need to be prepared for the one out of ten that does reach you. Be in a positive frame of mind, have your badge of courage on, make sure the light of hope is shining brightly, have your strength at the highest level, be determined, and don't lose faith! One in ten is not bad at all. Those numbers are in your favor!

DAY 141

I've heard there are troubles of more than one kind; some come from ahead and some come from behind. But I've brought a big bat. I'm all ready, you see; now my troubles are going to have troubles with me.
—Dr. Seuss, 1904-1991
German-American Author

What does your big bat consist of? Your bat consists of courage, faith, hope, determination, inner strength, love, happiness, and it's branded: "Cancer Slugger". Make sure you have your "cancer slugger" with you at all times on your journey. There will be troubles ahead and behind. When they see your big "cancer slugger", your troubles will know they are going to have troubles with you!

DAY 142

To live without hope is to cease to live.
—Fyodor Dostoevsky, 1821-1881
Russian Novelist

Never lose hope! Even on the hardest of days. Hope is the air in your lungs! According to psychologytoday.com, "hope allows people to approach problems with a mindset and strategy-set suitable to success, thereby increasing the chances they will actually accomplish their goals." Hope can do wonders even if you have lost everything in life. Your hope makes you strong. Remember that with hope, you have to have effort to reach that hope. Be patient and don't lose hope!

DAY 143

I will keep America moving forward, always forward, for a better America, for an endless enduring dream and a thousand points of light. This is my mission and I will complete it.
—George H. W. Bush, 1924-present
41st President of the United States

You will keep yourself moving forward, always forward, for a better you, for an endless enduring dream and a thousand points of light. This is your mission and you will complete it. We know you can do it!

DAY 144

We are twice armed if we fight with faith.
—Plato, 427 BC-347 BC
Greek Philosopher

Keep your faith in yourself strong. Keep faith in your hopes and dreams. Keep faith in your team. Keep faith in your plan for the journey. Faith nourishes the heart and soul. Without faith, you cannot expect things to turn out alright for yourself. There is a level if importance to having faith, a high level.

As wanderlustworker.com puts it, "Faith is an important element to all human life on earth. Life is precious, but it can also be remarkably difficult at times. Faith is what helps to get us through, illuminating the pathway in times of darkness, helping to give us strength in times of weakness. Without faith, we are nothing."

Be twice armed in your battle with cancer; fight with faith!

DAY 145

Cheerfulness keeps up a kind of daylight in the mind and fills it with steady and perpetual serenity.
—Joseph Addison, 1672-1719
English Poet

Some days with your cancer, cheerfulness seems like it is not an option. That is when you need it the most! Let it bring daylight to your mind, which is dark and clouded over from the stress and pain of that day. Let serenity settle in and wash the negative thoughts and pain away. If you are a grandparent, call your grandkid. That will always bring you cheerfulness. If you're not and you're a parent, call and talk to your kids. You can also watch your favorite movie. You could listen to your favorite music. Sit by the window and watch the birds and squirrels play. Do something you love and you'll find that cheerfulness is settling in and pushing the cancer stress out!

DAY 146

To have courage for whatever comes in life—everything lies in that.
—Saint Teresa of Avila, 1515-1582
Roman Catholic Saint

Again, a reminder of courage and the important role it plays in life. Especially in your life with cancer! Courage is like a call to action for you. A call to stand up and fight cancer face to face. Each day of life is precious, so for you, the importance of making courageous choices today is even more poignant. Don't wait 'til tomorrow or the next day. Be courageous today and every day! Wear your badge of courage proudly all day, every day!

DAY 147

Fear connotes something that interferes with what you're doing.
—John Glenn, 1921-2016
American Astronaut & Senator

Don't let fear interfere with your journey. Senator Glenn knows all about fear. You know he must have had some fear when he flew the Friendship 7 Mission to become the first American to orbit the earth. He did not let the fear of boarding a rocket and riding into space stop him. His courage squashed out the fear and he instantly became an American hero. He also overcame fear at the age of 77 when he returned to space on the Space Shuttle Discovery, becoming the oldest person to fly into space.

Use your courage to keep fear out of your way on this journey. You don't need any interference as you push ahead. For you, time is precious. Don't let anything interfere with your goal of completing your mission, just as Senator Glenn finished his missions. You too, would be an American hero for doing so!

DAY 148

Put your heart, mind, and soul into even your smallest acts. This is the secret to success.
—Swami Sivananda, 1887-1963
Hindi Spiritual Teacher

Your acts are not small on this journey. They are large and of upmost importance. This still applies to them, of course. You must put forth an effort in order to be successful on this journey. You cannot sit on the sidelines and watch cancer do whatever it wants. You need to get out there and face it using your heart, mind, and soul. Success does not come easy and success on this journey will be very hard. Remember though, your success comes from the effort put forth and not the ultimate outcome. Jim and Julie both had successful journeys even though the ultimate outcome was their death.

DAY 149

Much of what we call evil... can often be converted into a bracing and tonic good by a simple change of the sufferer's inner attitude from one of fear to one of fight.
—William James, 1842-1910
American Philosopher

Yes, we call cancer the *evil* beast. Let that fear boiling in you produce some great courage. The courage that will change your attitude and allow you to fight the evil beast. You have all the tools, all the weapons, all army, all the knowledge, and all faith needed for this battle. You can do it! We are here for you!

DAY 150

Let us make our future now and let us make our dreams tomorrow's reality.
—Malala Yousafzai, 1997-present
Pakistani Activist

These awesome, uplifting words from a young 20-year-old who continues to make her dreams reality today. At a very young age she started fighting for the rights of women and children to attend school. The Taliban in her home area in

Pakistan banned females from attending school. Her advocacy grew into an international movement. Her advocacy became so strong, the Taliban were threatened by it. On October 9, 2012 a Taliban gunman tried to assassinate her. She was hit, but survived. "She became the most famous teenager in the world," said journalist Deutsche Welle. In 2014 she became the youngest person ever to win the Nobel Peace Prize. She made her future now and her dreams became reality.

You, too can make your future now! You, too, can make your dreams tomorrow's reality! Make the effort and be determined to make it happen. The only person that can stop you is you. So off you go; go chase down your dreams and bring them to reality!

DAY 151

If you always put a limit on everything you do, physical or anything else, it will spread into your work and into your life. There are no limits. There are only plateaus and you must not stay there; you must go beyond them.
—Bruce Lee, 1940-1973
Chinese-American Actor

You will reach many plateaus on this journey of yours. Don't mistake them for a comfortable place to stick around in. You must continue to push ahead. Consider those plateaus as rungs on a ladder. Keep climbing to the top. At the top of this ladder, you will find what you're looking for.

DAY 152

It is in your moments of decision that your destiny is shaped.
—Tony Robbins, 1960-present
American Author

Make your decision on how you are going to handle the cancer diagnosis. That decision will shape your destiny. How do you want your destiny to play out? Your choice to go ahead with this journey will shape your destiny positively. You cannot give up along the way or linger with doubt. By doing so, you may alter that destiny in a negative manner.

DAY 153

Reach for it. Push yourself as far as you can.
—Christa McAuliffe, 1948-1986

American Astronaut & Teacher

Reach for it. "Christa," as her mom said shortly before the Space Shuttle Challenger was to take off, "she has always reached for the stars!" She pushed as far as she could to be selected as the first teacher that would go to space over 11,000 other teachers. She did it; she pushed herself right to the stars aboard the Challenger. Tragedy struck shortly after the Challenger lifted off and blasted towards space. The Challenger exploded, killing all 7 aboard.

President Ronald Reagan said it best: "The crew of the space shuttle Challenger honored us by the manner in which they lived their lives. We will never forget them, nor the last time we saw them, this morning, as they prepared for their journey and waved goodbye and 'slipped the surly bonds of earth' to 'touch the face of God.'"

Christa's journey was still successful. She reached for her dreams and made it happen. Her journey did not have a happy ending, but that does not make it unsuccessful. You need to reach for it on your journey. Push yourself as far as you can to complete your journey with cancer. By your effort and attitude alone, you make this journey successful. Jim and Julie had successful journeys, but they also slipped the surly bonds of earth to touch the face of God. Whether a happy or sad ending to your journey, know that you are a success. Nobody can take that away from you!

DAY 154

As people are walking all the time, in the same spot, a path appears.
—John Locke, 1632-1704
English Philosopher

Many have walked before you on this journey. Talk to a cancer survivor and learn from his or her experience. It could be very valuable for you. It may save many heartaches you could have along the way. Of course, ask where that path begins. Follow the path made for you to reach your final and glorious destination.

DAY 155

In one's self lies the whole world and if you know how to look and learn, the door is there and the key is in your hand. Nobody on earth can give you either the key or the door to open, except yourself.
—Jiddu Krishnamurti, 1895-1986
Indian Philosopher

Look at what lies ahead of you. Learn from your physicians and caretakers. The door that leads you to cancer freedom is before you and you have the key. Only you can decide to unlock it and proceed. Do it with confidence and courage. You are not alone when you enter through that door. We all are with you! This new world with cancer you are entering can be scary and difficult at times. Remember these items as you on your journey in this new world: number one, you have a great team around you to support and help you. Number two, you won't be in this "cancer" world forever. Don't get discouraged; stay positive and push on through.

DAY 156

Life is like riding a bicycle. To keep your balance, you must keep moving.
 —Albert Einstein, 1879-1955
 German Theoretical Physicist

You do not want to lose your balance while on your journey with cancer and fall. If you do, cancer could catch you. You must keep peddling to maintain your balance and stay on your path straight ahead. *Essential Life Skills* makes it pretty clear: "We tend to underestimate how much maintaining balance contributes to living life successfully and productively." On your journey, you must maintain a balance of courage, faith, hope, attitude, sleep/rest, good nutrition, and determination. If any of these are missing or out of balance, cancer could overcome you.

So, keep your balance by peddling straight ahead without stopping. Keep pushing on!

DAY 157

Smile in the mirror. Do that every morning and you'll start to see a big difference in your life.
—Yoko Ono, 1933-present
Japanese Singer-Songwriter

Doing this will give you a dose of good medicine to start your day. Let it make a difference for you on your daily journey with cancer. Your happiness is very much a key to your future success. What better to start a day than a smile back to yourself. Maybe even smile and say, "I can do this!" Each day is very important for you, so make sure to look at that beautiful person each morning!

DAY 158

To succeed in life, you need three things: a wishbone, a backbone, and a funny bone.

—Reba McEntire, 1955-present
American Singer-Songwriter

To succeed on your journey with cancer, you need all three of these as well. Let your wishbone carry your faith, hope, and courage. Your backbone will hold you up on those hard days when you have little strength and energy. The key to your backbone is to keep your attitude positive and your outlook positive. Doing that keeps your backbone firm and strong, so it can carry a heavy load. Your funny bone is to keep you in good spirits throughout your journey. Laughter and happiness are strong medications for you that must be taken daily. Make sure not to misplace your funny bone; you need it daily!

DAY 159

Whenever there is a human being there is a chance for a kindness.
—Seneca, 4 BC-65 AD
Roman Philosopher

Kindness is something you will need as well, as you travel down this path with cancer. There is nothing better than on day when you are feeling low, a friend pops in to see you and brings with them a big wheelbarrow of kindness. Perks you right up and puts a smile on your face. That is why it is so important to have a good team around you. You need them and you really need what they bring to you. Don't ever think or assume that you can travel this path alone. You will never make it to the end without a solid team supporting you! Bringing you kindness and love that makes your path clear.

DAY 160

> *Life is full of beauty. Notice it. Notice the bumble bee, the small child, and the smiling faces. Smell the rain and feel the wind. Live your life to the fullest potential and fight for your dreams.*
> —Ashley Smith, 1978-present
> American Author

Take note of the beauty around you. Let it bring warmth to your soul and fuel for your strength, determination and courage. Try to live each day in beauty to help you fight for your dream of being cancer-free.

Julie used to sit by the window in her bedroom at the house we grew up in. The neighbors had a nut tree right outside her window. She would notice the beauty, the squirrels playing and eating nuts, and the birds flying in and out of that tree. On summer days she would have that window open to smell the scents of summer: the cut grass, the blooming flowers, and the approaching rain storm. She would also listen to the beautiful sounds of summer, the birds singing, her dog Gus barking, the neighbor kids playing, and the grass being cut. She noticed the beauty in life; she was beauty in life and death.

DAY 161

I decided to fly through the air and live in the sunlight and enjoy life as much as I could.
—Evel Knievel, 1938-2007
American Stunt Performer

Let your mind fly through the air with the birds and live your life on the rays of the sunshine. Enjoy your life the best you can and it will make your journey much easier.

I think Jim and Evel were long lost brothers. Jim flew through the air and lived in the sunlight and made sure he enjoyed his life. I have a picture hanging in my office of Jim riding a motorcycle through a wall of fire. He autographed the picture for my son, Cody. It reads: "Cody, lead a normal life. Love, Uncle Jim" The funny part is *normal life*. Is riding a motorcycle in a stunt show a normal life? What Jim was telling Cody was to enjoy your life your way that is normal to you. Do what makes you happy. We also have a picture of Jim on his first motorcycle with all of us kids. I am four years old in this picture sitting on the gas tank looking up to Jim on the driver's seat. I always looked up to him; he was my own personal Evel Knievel!

DAY 162

> Every Luke Skywalker needs his Darth Vader.
> —Paul Di Flippo, 1954-present
> American Writer

Cancer is your Darth Vader. It's evil, it's dark, and it wants to kill you. Be like Luke Skywalker and battle your Darth Vader to the bitter end. Use your lightsaber as your weapon. It is a very powerful saber made up of your courage, faith, hope, determination, and love. Strike him down with this. The force is strong in you!

DAY 163

> When you have confidence, you can have a lot of fun. And when you have fun, you can do amazing things.
> —Joe Namath, 1943-present
> American Professional Football Player

Have complete confidence in yourself that you can complete this journey. Then you can have fun along the way. That fun equals happiness and that happiness is a very important medication for you. When you're happy and having fun, you feel full of energy and can do amazing things. The amazing thing for you is defeating cancer. Do this and people will be talking about your amazing feat for years to come!

DAY 164

> *Life is one big road with lots of signs. So, when you're riding through the ruts, don't complicate your mind. Flee from hate, mischief, and jealousy. Don't bury your thoughts; put your vision to reality. Wake up and live!*
> —Bob Marley, 1945-1981
> Jamaican Singer-Songwriter

This journey you are on will take you on those rough roads with ruts and potholes. Don't let your mind get clouded up with negative thoughts. Let your mind tend to what's at hand right now, your cancer. Worrying about other things only blocks your vision. The vision you need to see the path of your journey clearly. Wake up and complete your journey!

DAY 165

Have you had a kindness shown? Pass it on; 'twas not given for thee alone. Pass it on; let it travel down the years, let it wipe another's tears, 'til in heaven the deed appears—pass it on.
—Henry Burton, 1578-1648
English Puritan

I love this quote from Mr. Burton. The whole world needs more of this. When a member of your team passes kindness unto you, make sure to pass it on to another as well. It needs to be one big continuous circle. You know how important kindness is to you. A strong medication that you need to take daily. It is also important for others. Don't soak it in all to yourself. Share it with others; it will be back tomorrow for your daily dose.

DAY 166

Some days there won't be a song in your heart. Sing anyway.
—Emory Austin
American Motivational Speaker

You will have those days on this journey that there is no song in your heart, no strength in your body, no smile on your face, no giddy up in your step, no happiness in your soul, and no sunshine in your mind. Those days you have to push and will yourself to find what can turn that all around, so you can sing, anyway. Something to cheer you up and make the pain disappear. Put your favorite music on and sing along with it. Lose yourself in those songs and let everything slip away for a little while.

DAY 167

Become a possibilitarian. No matter how dark things seem to be or actually are, raise your sights and see possibilities—always see them, for they're always there.

—Norman Vincent Peale, 1898-1993
American Author

Things do get dark at times along your journey. If you raise your sights above that cancer you can see the possibilities to overcome it. Just by doing that, you are halfway home. If you don't see the possibilities, you are trying too hard, like not seeing the trees because the forest is in the way. Just relax, close your eyes, breathe, and look again. There you will see the possibilities and now is the time to act on them!

DAY 168

When it rains, look for rainbows. When it's dark, look for stars.
                    —Oscar Wilde, 1854-1900
                                Irish Poet

The Irish do like their rainbows! Here is the age-old question; is the glass half full or half empty? How will you answer that question is key to how successful your journey will be. Hopefully you are trying to find the rainbows, the stars, the pot of gold, the moon, the leprechaun, the sun, and all the good positive things! By the way, the glass is always half full!

DAY 169

The game of life is a lot like football. You have to tackle your problems, block your fears, and score your points when you get the opportunity.
                    —Lewis Grizzard, 1946-1994
                                American Writer

Keep your fears blocked at the line of scrimmage with courage. Every time that cancer tries to grab the ball and take control of the game, tackle him. Don't let him get any first downs. Don't let him intercept any of your passes. Don't let him cause you to fumble the ball. Keep control of the ball and you can do all the scoring and come out victorious over him. The line in Vegas has you favored by a spread of seven and a half. Cover the spread and send cancer packing.

DAY 170

Hold fast to dreams, for if dreams die, life is a broken-winged bird that cannot fly.
—Langston Hughes, 1902-1967
American Poet

Our country was built on dreams and continues to grow on dreams. Many before us have held fast to dreams to make it possible for us to dream. They didn't let go at all costs. Look to our founding fathers and all revolutionary soldiers that brought us freedom from the monarchy of England. Many died holding onto that dream. Look at Abraham Lincoln and his dream to end slavery. The Northern army believed in this and held fast to it as they fought; again, many died with that dream still clutched in their hands. Look at the Wright Brothers who had the dream that man could fly. Look at President Kennedy and his dream for a man to walk on the moon. Look at President Reagan and his dream to end the Cold War. His famous speech at the Berlin Wall, "Mr. Gorbachev, tear down this wall!'

Hold fast to your dream of beating cancer. It may come with setbacks, pain, and suffering, but don't let go. You don't want a broken wing; you want to fly again, healthy and happy!

DAY 171

Courage is not having the strength to go on; it is going on when you don't have the strength.
—Theodore Roosevelt, 1858-1919
26th President of the United States

The days you are weak and can't get out of bed, but you do—that is courage. The days you are sick from chemotherapy and still go in and get another dose. That is courage. The days you don't have strength to make the family dinner, but you do. That is courage. The days you can't do much and still go to your kid's game. That is courage. The day you said, "Cancer won't get me." That is courage. The day you started to battle cancer. That is courage. The day you said, "I won't give up." That is courage. The day you told your family and loved ones that you have cancer. That is courage.

You are going on when you don't have the strength. Don't let anyone ever say that you don't have courage!

DAY 172

It is during our darkest moments that we must focus to see the light.
—Aristotle, 384 BC-322 BC
Greek Philosopher

There is light at the end of your tunnel. Some days it may be very hard to see, but it is there. If you focus hard with all your faith, all your hope, all your determination, all your courage, and an open mind that is thinking positively, you will see it. Some days you just have to push and work harder than others to see through the darkness, the pain, the weakness, and clouds of negativity. Each day try to make that light a little brighter in your eyes 'til one day the end of the tunnel has been reached and you can feel the rays on light upon your face.

DAY 173

I've had to learn to fight all my life—got to learn to keep smiling. If you smile, things will work out.
—Serena Williams, 1981-present
American Professional Tennis Player

I would say that this philosophy works out pretty well. Serena is pretty good proof of it. Just look at her career numbers: 23 Grand Slam titles in singles play (world record), 14 Grand Slam titles in women mixed doubles, two Grand Slam titles in mixed doubles, one Olympic gold medal in singles play, three Olympic gold medals in women doubles play, 72 WTA titles and a winning percentage of 78%. Many sports journalists say she is the greatest female athlete in the world. Hard to argue those numbers.

You are in the fight of your life. Try a little of Serena's philosophy and keep smiling. Things will work out!

DAY 174

> *I feel like life is really short and it's important to enjoy yourself and embrace whatever comes your way; whether it's a challenging day or a great day, just welcome it with open arms. No matter who you are, you can't escape challenges; they are part of life.*
> —Miranda Kerr, 1983-present
> Australian Model

Yes, life is really short! Every day does bring new challenges and especially for you in your situation. This challenge proves to be very difficult and may be lengthy. Something you don't want to head off into alone and think you will be successful. Your team is with you; don't forget that and don't leave them behind. You cannot escape this challenge, so you may as well embrace it with open arms and determination. Let your courage, faith, and hope take over on this journey.

DAY 175

When you encourage others, you in the process are encouraged because you're making a commitment and difference in that person's life. Encouragement really does make a difference.
—Zig Ziglar, 1926-2012
American Author

You are a part of this encouragement circle of life. Your team will be giving you encouragement throughout this journey. It will make a difference in your journey and it will make a difference for those giving you this encouragement. With them making a difference in your journey, they feel encouraged and that triggers more encouragement back onto you. A nice, big circle of life. Some of the encouragement you may receive could be like this: "Can I hug you?" "I love you." "I am praying for you." "Nothing I can say will make this better, but I am here for you always." "I am sending you positive thoughts." "You are my hero." "I'm proud of you." "God loves you."

"Cancer started the fight, but you are going to finish it." "Here is my shoulder; it's okay to cry."

You have many people behind you; be open to all their encouragement!

DAY 176

Into each life some rain must fall.
—Henry W. Longfellow, 1807-1882
American Poet

The rain is falling in your life right now. Some days it is falling hard. Put your raincoat on and pop open your umbrella. Don't let this rain slow you down on your journey. Keep pushing straight ahead down that long, narrow path. Don't be distracted by anything and slip and fall in the mud. As you end this journey, the rain will let up, the sunshine will break through and a beautiful rainbow will appear.

DAY 177

In everyone's life, at some point, our inner fire goes out. It is then burst into flame by an encounter with another human being. We should all be thankful for those people who rekindle the inner spirit.
—Albert Schweitzer, 1875-1965
French-German Theologian

Someone on your team is that person that will rekindle your inner fire. It could be your physician, your spiritual leader, your best friend, your mother, your daughter, your brother. Someone close to you will do that for you. You need to use the words of *The Doors* and Jim Morrison, "Come on, baby, light my fire." You may need that fire within rekindled several times during your journey. Keep your team close; you don't know when you may need them.

Fr. Edward Petty would come visit Julie during her journey. I remember that they would have long private talks. Mom used to tell me to, "leave them alone; they need to talk." It seemed after these visits Julie was more upbeat and ready to go. Things were bleak that last summer, but when Fr. Ed visited, things seemed better all the way around.

You can't just pick this person. It will just happen and you will feel it within you. Your inner fire burning again.

DAY 178

Continuous effort — not strength or intelligence — is the key to unlocking our potential.
—Winston Churchill, 1874-1965
British Prime Minister

Keep pushing; don't let up. There will be days where your strength is lacking; just give the best effort you can. That daily effort will unlock your complete potential for your victory over cancer. Churchill knows this because he lived it as Prime Minister of Britain during World War II. The British were completely outnumbered by the German Luftwaffe. During the Blitz, Germany's continuous attack on England, London was bombed by air for 56 out of 57 days and nights in the fall of 1940. The British, led by Churchill, just kept giving a continuous effort day by day, night by night. The cities around them crumbling from the bombs of the Luftwaffe. Churchill laid the groundwork for this in a speech earlier that summer of 1940.

"We shall go on to the end. We shall fight in France, we shall fight on the seas and oceans, we shall fight with growing confidence and growing strength in the air, we shall defend our island, whatever the cost may be. We shall fight on the beaches, we shall fight on the landing grounds, we shall fight in the fields and in the streets, we shall fight in the hills; we shall never surrender."

Do as the British did; give the continuous effort. Close your eyes and think that Churchill is on your radio giving that speech directly to you. Say to yourself, "I shall fight at home, I shall fight in the yard and in the park, I shall fight with growing confidence and growing strength, I shall defend my body, whatever the cost may be. I shall fight at the hospital, I shall fight in the clinics, I shall fight in the fields and in the streets, I shall fight in the hills; I shall never surrender!"

DAY 179

You're never a loser until you quit trying.
—Mike Ditka, 1939—present
American Professional Football Coach

Don't ever quit trying! Don't be a loser. Nobody likes losers. Keep trying! Not all cancer patients will beat cancer, but that does not make them losers. They are champions because they never gave up and tried right up to the end. Anyone that makes an effort will never be given the label "loser".

None of these people that passed from cancer are losers and nobody should ever think so; my sister Julie, my brother Jim, my grandpa Charles, Father Edward Petty, Walter Payton, Patrick Swayze, Paul Newman, Peter Jennings, Farrah Fawcett, Ted Kennedy, Bob Denver "Gilligan", Vince Lombardi, Audrey Hepburn, Jack Lemmon, Milton Berle, John Wayne, Walt Disney, Dean Martin, Jackie Kennedy, Frank Sinatra, Dr. Seuss, Babe Ruth, Joe DiMaggio, Mickey Mantle, Roger Maris, Ulysses S. Grant, Sally

Ride, Humphrey Bogart, Sigmund Freud, Pope John XXIII, and Saint John Paul II. All of these people are champions. One is even a saint! All of these people can be looked up to for their courage and bravery. The word *quit* was not in their vocabulary. As it should not be in yours!

DAY 180

The Circle

Life is time
Time captured
Time shared
An intersection of time
A brief union of space
Time shared?
Time captured?
I am your memories;
You are my time.
    —Julie M. Avery, 1961-1982
    American Poet and Sister

Very well written, sister! Says it all! Julie wrote this for our family when she knew that her days with us were numbered. Thirty-five years later, I still can't read it without a tear in my eye. She will always be my memory and until we meet again, I will be her time.

DAY 181

My friends, love is better than anger. Hope is better than fear. Optimism is better than despair. So, let us be loving, hopeful, and optimistic. And we'll change the world.
—Jack Layton, 1950-2011
Canadian Politician

You want to change your world, a world without cancer within you. Accept our love for you and remain hopeful and optimistic. This can change your world. It's too late to have anger about this. It's time to take this journey with love and support from your team. Let the fear boil into courage and hope. Despair won't help you at all. It is a distraction you don't need and cannot afford. Instead, be optimistic and as positive as you can. You and your team can change your world. It will not be easy and it will not be fast. Be patient and don't ever lose hope!

DAY 182

Never die easy. Why run out of bounds and die easy? Make that linebacker pay. It carries

into all facets of your life. It's okay to lose, to die, but don't die without trying, without giving it your best.
—Walter Payton, 1954-1999
American Professional Football Player

That is why Walter Payton was and still is my favorite football player. He played the game just as he described. He was like many of the players these days that will run out of bounds instead of taking a hit from the opposing team. Walter and this style of play made him one of the greatest players in the history of the NFL. He played many years on a Chicago Bears team that was not very good. He learned how to lose with class and dignity. After he retired from football as the all-time leading rusher, he came down with a liver disease that led to bile duct cancer. He needed to put his style of football to work in his personal life, which he did very courageously. He gave it his best and never stopped trying. He lost that battle, but he did not die easy!

DAY 183

I warn you not to underestimate my powers.
—Mark Hamill, 1951-present
American Actor

This, of course, is a line from the Star Wars movie from Luke Skywalker. Mark Hamill played the role of Luke. As you go to bed each night, tell the evil beast, cancer, this! For your cancer is your Darth Vader, the dark and evil side. You have the characteristics of a Jedi Knight, just like Luke Skywalker. Vader knows not that you are a Jedi with the great powers of faith, hope, love, courage, determination, bravery, and positive thinking. Your Darth Vader has underestimated your powers. Strike him down! May the force be with you!

DAY 184

Even a happy life cannot be without a measure of darkness, and the word happy would lose its meaning if it were not balanced by sadness. It is far better to take things as they come along with patience and equanimity.
—Carl Jung, 1875-1961
Swiss Psychiatrist

Your happy life has been interrupted by the darkness of cancer. Reflect on those happy times to balance the sadness of cancer. It will help you each day. Be patient, have mental calmness and composure in this difficult time. It shall balance back to your favor.

In October of 2015 all of us Avery brothers came back to Dubuque to spend several days with Jim. We did not do a lot of activities. We spent most of our time reflecting on the happy times of years gone by. This brought Jim that balance back of happiness and sadness. You could see it in his eyes. It meant a great deal to him that we had this time together. I know it brought him calmness as well as he battled the last days after that visit. He was able to take that balance and mental calmness with him as he slipped away to the other side.

DAY 185

Don't ever doubt yourself or waste a second of your life. It's too short and you're too special.
—Ariana Grande, 1993-present
American Actress & Singer

Life is very short and for you, it seems even shorter. You do not want to waste any time. You need all of your time to battle this. Never doubt yourself about beating cancer. Hold on tight to your confidence! You can do this. You have courage and faith to make it happen. You have a great team supporting you that knows you are a special person and they are going to help as much as possible. Don't doubt yourself!

DAY 186

You take away all the other luxuries in life and if you can make someone smile and laugh, you have given the special gift: happiness.
—Brad Garrett, 1960-present
American Actor & Comedian

The importance of happiness again. You can't hear that enough during your journey. UC Berkeley did research on how happiness affects our health. They published some of the results in *Greater Good Magazine*. They listed six ways happiness is good for your health. Here they are:

1. Happiness protects your heart. Happiness predicts lower heart rates and blood pressure.
2. Happiness strengthens your immune system. Research is finding a link between happiness and a stronger immune system.
3. Happiness combats stress. Stress triggers biological changes in our hormones and blood pressure. Happiness seems to temper these effects and may recover more quickly.
4. Happy people have fewer aches and pains. Positive emotion mitigates pain in the context of disease.

5. Happiness combats disease and disability. Happiness is associated with improvements in more severe, long-term conditions as well, not just shorter-term aches and pains.
6. Happiness lengthens our lives. The happest-seeming people lived 7-10 years longer than the least happy.

Let your team make you smile and laugh! The results could help you more than you think!

DAY 187

A dream is what makes people love life even when it is painful.
—Theodore Zeldin, 1933-present
American Scholar

Make beating your cancer the dream that drives you. The dream that makes you love life each day because you are going to battle that cancer again today to make for a much better tomorrow. Keep that thought process every day, even those painful days. This dream fulfilled will let you dream much bigger dreams for yourself and future!

DAY 188

A will finds a way.
 —Orison Swett Marden, 1848—1924
 American Author

We all have heard this quote before. Well, now we know who penned it. Don't lose your will during this journey. Keep it strong and well fed. Your will likes to eat positive thoughts, self-determination, courage, bravery, and optimism. Let your will find your way down the path of your journey. You will need to rely on it when that path narrows and winds through the dark. The journey is long and hard; make sure to keep your will fed so it doesn't weaken on you.

DAY 189

Fear of failure: it's the greatest motivational tool. It drives me and drives me and drives me.
 —Jerry West, 1938-present
 American Professional Basketball Player

Fear of failure is natural and it is okay. The stakes are much higher for you than a basketball player in a game. As we have said before, let that fear grow your courage. The courage you will need each day to get out of bed and battle this cancer. The courage to look that cancer straight in the eye and say, "Not today!" The courage to fight on when you feel you can't. Wear your badge of courage with great price so everyone can see it!

DAY 190

Always do your best. What you plant now, you will harvest later.
       —Og Mandio, 1923-1996
       American Author

Do your best today and your best tomorrow will be easier. Doing your best every day against cancer is planting the seeds for a healthy you. Keep planting those seeds daily. You cannot have enough fields planted with them. If you have a hundred acres or a thousand acres, keep planting those seeds. You hope to have a bountiful harvest at the end of this journey.

DAY 191

Heavy hearts, like heavy clouds in the sky, are best relieved by the letting of a little water.
     —Christopher Morley, 1890-1957
       American Poet

It's perfectly fine to cry and perfectly good to cry. You can't let all that water back up. All your team members have two shoulders. Find just one and relieve your heavy heart and pain. Let the pain and the heaviness of your heart wash away down your cheeks. The sun will shine on you again after this rain shower, bringing a rainbow of hope for better days ahead.

DAY 192

> *One of the best ways to make yourself happy in the present is to recall happy times from the past. Photos are a great memory—prompt, and because we tend to take photos of happy occasions, they weight our memories to the good.*
> —Gretchen Rubin, 1965-present
> American Author

Throughout our childhood my father would take movies of special family events. He took them on an old 8mm camera. So, we had spools and spools of family movies. We pulled those movies out several times during Julie's journey. We would watch them and have such a good time. There is one movie we all loved the best that made us laugh so hard. Dad was filming our brother Mike roller skating down the sidewalk in the back yard. He got his legs twisted up a fell down. We would reverse the film and replay several times. It was just as funny backwards as forwards. We played it so many times we burned that part of the 8mm film. Well, those movies made Julie very happy during some of the difficult days she had. She had a big old smile on her face watching those happy memories.

Hopefully you have old photo books you can look through and have the same reactions. Better yet, maybe you have old family movies like we did. Let those lighten up the weight of your pain and suffering and bring a smile to that beautiful face. You will feel energized afterwards.

DAY 193

I follow three rules: Do the right thing, do the best you can, and always show people you care.
—Lou Holtz, 1937-present
American College & Pro Football Coach

You, too should follow these three rules: do the right thing—fight like hell to beat cancer, do the best you can—don't give up or give in, continue straight ahead, and always show people you care. When they see you care, they come to your side and help you in this battle, they join your army and bear arms to fight this evil beast. Caring is very contagious and wins people over. I was told to do the best I can. If not, it must not have been worth doing. For you, it is very worthy of doing—doing your best to save your time here with us!

DAY 194

You either get bitter or you get better. It's that simple. You either take what has been dealt to you and allow it to make you a better person, or you allow it to tear you down. The choice does not belong to fate, it belongs to you.
—Josh Shipp, 1982-present
American Author

For those of you who like it black and white with no rose petals to make it feel good, there you go. Right to the point advice. No sugar coating on this one. Shipp is right, though. The choice is yours and yours alone. When you made the choice to fight this battle, you took the first steps of making yourself a better person. By journey's end, you will be surprised at your personal growth. If you stop or hesitate for a long time, this will tear you down. Keep making the good choices along this journey!

DAY 195

Bravery is the capacity to perform properly even when scared half to death.
—Omar Bradley, 1893-1981
American Army General

How does one perform properly when battling cancer? You give it your best effort. You stay positive during the battle. You keep your faith and hope at high levels. You stay optimistic. You stay determined. You rely on help from your team. You let your fear turn into courage. You don't get distracted. You stay the course. You stay calm, cool, and collected. You are brave, very brave. General Omar Bradley would be proud to have you in his army.

Jim and Julie both were so very brave. The long term outlook for both of them at the time of their diagnosis was not the best. They both still give it their best. They performed "properly" even though they were scared half to death those first few days. The best thing they both did was to stay calm, cool, and collected. This made things much easier for the rest of our family. To do that alone is great bravery.

DAY 196

Our greatest glory is not in never failing, but in rising every time we fall.
—Confucius, 551 BC-479 BC
Chinese Philosopher

During your journey you will fall. You will fall more than once and more than twice. Rise each time to battle another day. Don't let this cancer think he has gotten the best of you. For he has not even seen the best of you yet. Ride that glory, like wind behind a sail, straight ahead down your journey's path.

Look at the Chicago Cubs. They were knocked down for 108 years in a row. Every spring they were right back up on their feet to battle again year after year after year. Not only did the team get back up each year, their fans crawled up off the ground and stood again to battle. Then finally in 2016 they rode their glory back to a World Championship. Making it one of the most glorious championships in the history of baseball. If the Chicago Cubs can do it, you surely can!

By the way, the last paragraph was hard to write. I am a huge St. Louis Cardinal fan!

DAY 197

When a resolute young fellow steps up to the great bully, the world, and takes him boldly by the beard, he is often surprised to find it comes off in his hand, and that it was only tied on to scare away timid adventurers.
—Ralph Waldo Emerson, 1803-1882
American Poet

Be a resolute cancer patient and step up to the great bully, cancer, grab him boldly by his beard and pull it off. Exposing him for the creep he is. He now knows that he cannot scare you. That you are going to give him a very hard battle 'til journey's end. Cancer is what cancer is. Don't be afraid to step right up to him. His bark is worse than his bite. Have confidence that you can handle him.

DAY 198

To believe is to be strong. Doubt cramps energy. Belief is power.
—Frederick Robertson, 1816-1853
English Divine

Keep the belief that you can beat cancer. That belief will give you strength and power to battle on. Remember that your journey is long, don't lose belief. You need that strength and power throughout. As soon as any doubt settles in, it soaks up your energy and strength. We all have belief in you that will remain constant through your journey.

DAY 199

In life, as in a football game, the principle to follow is: hit the line hard; don't foul and don't shirk, but hit the line hard.
—Theodore Roosevelt, 1858-1919
26th President of the United States

Use this same philosophy when you are fighting your cancer. Give it all you have and hit the line hard. You have a great team on the field to help and support you. Keep using this philosophy day after day with your team. This will give you (well, should give you) victories each day of this long season, journey. Ride the momentum all the way to the Super Bowl.

DAY 200

All the animals except man know that the principal business of life is to enjoy it.
—Samuel Butler, 1835-1902
English Novelist

You ever just sit and watch squirrels run and play? Always having fun and enjoying their life. How about dogs at the dog park? My Fletcher just loved going to the dog park and being able to play with dogs. They just have a grand old time. We just need to figure this out. For you, enjoyment in life is hard. For you, enjoyment in life is very important. You need to enjoy your life as much as you can. This will give you happiness, which will give you strength, which will give you confidence, which will give you the courage to fight on. Find enjoyment in your life! Do what gives you that; go to the movies, take a long weekend away, go to a play, go visit your grandchildren, go to a concert—just find enjoyment!

DAY 201

Do what you feel in your heart to be right—for you'll be criticized anyway. You'll be damned if you do, and damned if you don't.
—Eleanor Roosevelt, 1884-1962
Former First Lady of the United States

Carry this attitude with you during your journey. Do what is best for you and your happiness. Don't worry about what people will think. Your happiness is key to beating down your cancer. So, if skydiving makes you happy, do it! If getting a tattoo makes you happy, do it! If getting your ears pierced makes you happy, do it! If telling off the wall jokes makes you happy, do it! If shaving your head bald makes you happy, do it! Who cares what others think? Do what you feel is right for you!

DAY 202

The confidence which we have in ourselves gives birth to much of that which we have in others.
—Francois De La Rochefoucauld, 1613-1680
          French Author

Confidence is contagious. You show your confidence every day you get up and continue on your journey with that darn cancer. When you do that day after day, your team sees and feels your confidence. Thus, their confidence in you and this journey rise to new levels. They are then better equipped to help you and support you. Then you can have all the confidence in the world in them. That they will be there for you.

  Jim showed great confidence during his journey, which gave me more confidence in myself and in him. Because of that, I would do anything I could to help him: cut his grass, sweep the shop up, sit with him during chemo treatments, run errands for him, and just sit and talk with him. I know this gave Jim much greater confidence in me, that I would be there for him. That I would be there for his "wife". That I would be there for our Mother and Father.

Be *confident*!

DAY 203

Do not squander time, for that is the stuff life is made of.
— Benjamin Franklin, 1706-1790
A Founding Father of the United States

This is even more important for you. Your time is precious. Use it wisely. Do not squander any of it. Use every minute you have to battle your cancer. When you squander any time at all, that time goes right into your cancer's back pocket. Cancer will use that time to do more damage to you and possible spread in you. Do not allow cancer to get any time at all. Use it all up yourself!

DAY 204

Do unto others as you would have others do unto you.
— Jesus Christ, 7 BC-30 AD
God's only Begotten Son

You need a lot of support from your team. Make sure you do unto them as you would have them do unto you. Show them love, kindness, fellowship, encouragement, positive thoughts, and commitment. Hopefully you receive these right back from them. This is what fuels your fire and brings you daily strength to battle on another day. This is the "Golden Rule" that all mankind needs to follow. Similar to this, Jesus tells his prophets to "love one another as I have loved you." You should also carry these thoughts of love with you as well. You need, your team needs and all of us need to love one another!

DAY 205

> *It has been my observation that most people get ahead during the time that others waste.*
> —Henry Ford, 1863-1947
> American Captain of Industry

For you, getting ahead is battling cancer every day and not losing ground to it. If you waste time, like has been mentioned before, that wasted time goes right to the cancer, so it can gain more strength and do more damage. Your time is very precious. There is none to waste. Make use of it the best you can by staying positive, enjoying life, finding happiness, sharing love, and sharing memories. So much to do! So, get to it!

DAY 206

Be the reason someone smiles today!
— Christopher Rivas
Latino Actor & Author

Making someone smile just simply feels good. Gives you that warm fuzzy feeling inside of you. Best part is that when you make someone smile, it makes you smile as well. It's one big dose of anti-cancer medication! Here are *Benefits Bridge's* top seven benefits from smiling:

1. Improved mood; smiling can boost your mood when you're feeling blue.
2. Lower blood pressure; smiling and laughing lowers blood pressure.
3. Stress relief; helps your body deal with stressful situations more effectively.
4. Better relationships; people who smile are perceived to be more likeable.
5. Stronger immune function; believe it or not, smiling and laughter boost your immune system.

6. Pain relief; the Mayo Clinic reports that laughter with smiling increases your pain threshold.
7. Longer life; a 2010 study shows that smiling and positive emotions are associated with increased life spans.

What more reasons do you need to smile?

DAY 207

Stay positive even when it seems like your life is falling apart.
—Unknown

This is hard in your situation with cancer, but it reaps many rewards if you can. Staying positive sets the tone for your whole journey. Being negative and pissed off about the situation will do no good at all and will give you negative results. It's okay to be mad and pissed off when you first learn of your cancer. That is natural. You just cannot carry that with you on the journey. It will have disastrous results. After your initial shock, take a deep breath and calm yourself. Ask yourself how you are going to get the best results out of this. This is the same when during the journey you get a bad check-up report. Go ahead and get mad. Then get right back on the positive train and continue on. This isn't easy, but it is necessary.

DAY 208

The first thing to learn in intercourse with others is noninterference with their own peculiar ways of being happy, provided those ways do not assume to interfere by violence with ours.
—Henry James, 1862-1916
American Author

Don't let anyone interfere with what makes you happy. Well, as long as you're not burning down the neighbors' house or something. Your happiness is key to your journey. You know that already! It cannot be said enough. As long as you're happy, those around you should be happy for you. Just for the heck of it, think of the most peculiar, odd, strange, and unusual thing that makes you happy and do It. See what kind of reaction you get. Hopefully everyone on your team will be happy about it, because you found happiness in it.

DAY 209

Time is shortening. But every day that I challenge this cancer and survive is a victory for me.
— Ingrid Bergman, 1915-1982
Swedish Actress

Every day that you wake up to greet the morning sun is a victory as well. Let that sunshine shine on your heart and soul to give you the courage and strength to get through that day. Take each small victory and let it build momentum for you to keep rolling along on your journey. Some days won't feel like victories, but they are. Each and every one of them! It is times like this you learn to live again. Just like the Foo Fighters song *Times Like These*.

It's times like these you learn to live again.
It's times like these you give and give again.
It's times like these you learn to love again.
It's times like these time and time again.

DAY 210

We have two options, medically and emotionally: give up or fight like hell.
— Lance Armstrong, 1971-present
Cancer Survivor

Say what you will about Lance, but he fought like hell against cancer and won. He also has raised millions upon millions of dollars for cancer research. Lance's light at the end of his tunnel was very dim. He had a very aggressive form of testicular cancer that by the time of his diagnosis it had spread to his lungs and brain. He never gave up, he never hesitated; he just pushed on ahead. Sticking to his physician's road map of the journey and allowing good support from his team. He did it; so can you! Fight like hell!

DAY 211

When you have exhausted all possibilities, remember this: you haven't.
—Thomas Edison, 1847-1931
American Inventor

There are always possibilities. Where would Thomas Edison be if he felt he exhausted all possibilities when he was inventing? We wouldn't have the light bulb, phonograph, movie camera, mimeograph, etc. Thomas Edison had 1093 patents when he passed away. He had many, many failures as well. Thomas Edison turned over every single leaf when he needed to. Like the sayings go:

There is more than one way to skin a cat.
There is more than one way to bake a cake.
There is more than one way to peel an orange.
There is more than one way to shine a penny.
There is more than one way to make a bed.

I think you get it. Don't give up. There is always a way!

DAY 212

Never be ashamed of a scar. It simply means you were stronger than whatever tried to hurt you.

—Unknown

Wear your scar with pride! You earned it! Let people see your bald head, your 12" scar, your one leg or whatever it may be. Let cancer know that you are stronger than him. He tried to hurt you, but you're trong. You're strong as nails!

I remember how strong Julie was. This quotation, I think, was written with her in mind. She wasn't the least bit timid about going out in public with her one leg shortly after amputation. She had a wig made, but when it was completed, she said she didn't need that. She won her "scars" as badges of courage. Giving her strength to fight on. She stood nose to nose with cancer.

DAY 213

How much time he gains who does not look to see what his neighbor says or does or thinks.
—Marcus Aurelius, 121AD-180AD
Roman Emperor

Time for you is so very precious. You need to gain time as well. Don't be distracted by anything that does not concern you. Take care of yourself and your family. It matters not what others are doing, saying, and thinking. Stay focused to what is at hand for you: cancer. Not only will you be more fulfilled doing so, you will have more energy to do so. Keep what is important to you at the forefront at all times. Don't take your eyes off cancer. If you do, he may bite.

DAY 214

Know what work you want to do and go after it. The young man that gets ahead must decide for himself what he wishes to do. Forms his own taste, his own enthusiasm, he must get

the motive and inspiration which are to start him on his way to a successful life.
—Alexander Graham Bell, 1847-1922
Scottish-American Inventor

What work do you want to do? Hopefully the work of battling cancer and hopefully you have already been battling it. You and you alone make that decision. Have the enthusiasm to do so. You have the best motive and inspiration to do this—*your life!* Gather up all your motivation, inspiration, enthusiasm and work at knocking cancer out.

If you have a terminal diagnosis of cancer, know what you want to accomplish and go do it. Live your bucket list, have fun and bring yourself happiness. Unfortunately, Jim and Julie received this diagnosis. They knew what they wanted and they worked to do it. I think their time with us was extended because they wanted to, needed to complete their bucket list.

DAY 215

Surround yourself with only people who are going to lift you higher.
—Oprah Winfrey, 1954-present
American Media Proprietor

This is of the upmost importance for you during the journey. I'm sure you realize that since I have mentioned it several times. Oprah is right on with this. Why waste your time and space with people who don't lift you up? Wouldn't life be better for everyone if we all did this and encourage others to do the same? Make sure all your team members are "uplifters"! If they are not, they shouldn't be in your circle. Negative people breed negative thoughts and vibes. Your cancer thrives on negativity. Don't let it thrive. Let your team lift you higher in positive vibes!

DAY 216

If you're not okay, that's okay. It will happen sometimes. But you have to tell yourself that things will be better tomorrow. Even if they're not better tomorrow, keep telling yourself they will be. Because eventually, tomorrow will be better.
—Samuel Miller, 1769-1850
American Theologian

Exactly right! Amazing that these words are over 200 years old and still ring true today. Look at your calendar. There are plenty of tomorrows on there. It will happen. That better tomorrow is somewhere on that calendar. Don't lose hope or faith. On that calendar are some more rough days as well. Just remember that this is a long journey with ups and downs. Take each day as it comes, knowing that tomorrow might be the best day.

DAY 217

It's the gymnasium of life where you get the workout, the resistance, and you find out things about yourself that you didn't know.
—Bishop T.D. Jakes, 1957-present
American Author

Battling cancer is the gymnasium of life. You definitely get a workout daily. You hope to get the resistance built up to battle another day. You will find out things about yourself that you did not know. You will find out you are braver then you thought. You will find out that you have more courage than you thought. You will find faith and hope growing in you each day. It may make you a better person. Lance Armstrong has said he is a better person now, after beating cancer, than he was prior to that. He also has said he is prouder of his victory over cancer than any of his cycling victories.

You are in the gymnasium every morning when you roll out of bed. Make sure you start your workout as soon as you roll out of bed as well.

DAY 218

You may have to fight the battle more than once to win it.
— Margaret Thatcher, 1925-2013
Former British Prime Minister

You may have to fight your battle with cancer more than once. You have to believe in yourself that you will be victorious. You must have patience. As long as there is time and as long as you put forth the effort, you are not defeated. Banish any negative thoughts you may have. This battle could come back after you have beaten it already. Be prepared for that possibility. Earn yourself the same title Margaret had, The Iron Lady. If you're a man, insert man and remove lady.

As you know from a previous hope message, Julie had to go to battle a second time. I am sure we all know several people that have had to go to battle a second and maybe third time with cancer. It is another ugly under side of this hideous disease!

DAY 219

Always remember you are braver than you believe, stronger than you seem, smarter than you think and loved more than you'll know.
—Christopher Robin, 1926-present
English Cartoon Character

I always knew as a child growing up watching *Winnie the Pooh* shows that Christopher Robin was a pretty smart kid. These words should be very special to you while you are battling cancer. These four words—braver, stronger, smarter and loved—give you what you need to battle daily. You are braver than you believe. You are just as brave as a Marine going into battle. Just as brave as a fireman rushing into a fire to save someone. Just as brave as a police officer in a stand out with a gunman. Yes, it's true! You all are willing to face down death and say, "Not today!" You are stronger than you seem. Reference back to my sister Julie. All of 100 pounds soaking wet, she didn't seem strong being that little, but she was the strongest person I ever met. You, too are much stronger than you think and seem. You are smarter than you think. Give yourself some credit here. You know what it is going to take to complete this journey. You know to follow the physician's road map. You know you cannot do this alone and need a good team around you. You know to stay positive, be determined, show courage, enjoy life, be happy, love and be loved, and be patient. You have a lot of people that love. More than you know. They will be there for you and with you. You can do this!

DAY 220

You are the stars and the world is watching you. By your presence, you send a message to every village, every city, every nation. A message of hope. A message of victory.
—Eunice Kennedy Shriver, 1921-2009
Founder of Special Olympics

These words from President Kennedy's sister were in a speech to the first athletes of the Special Olympics. She fought for inclusion her entire life for the mentally challenged. You can very well take these words and give them to all cancer patients. You are superstars for standing up to cancer. We are watching you, praying for you, and loving you. By standing up to cancer, you are sending a message to every village, every city, every nation. The message of hope. The message of victory. Remember your victory is not decided by the final outcome. Your victory is determined by how you get to the final outcome.

DAY 221

You can't calm the storm, so stop trying. What you can do is calm yourself. The storm will pass.
—Timber Hawkeye, 1977-present
Israeli Author

The storm you are in is a nasty storm. You need to stay calm throughout its entirety. Don't waste time and energy on getting upset or nervous. You have everything you need to get through this storm. You have your umbrella, your team. You have your raincoat, your courage. You have your rain boots, your strength and determination. You have your rain hat, your faith, and hope. Keep them on and use them. They will keep you dry from negativity and allow you to get to the end. And you know what follows a storm—your rainbow!

DAY 222

You gave us Viagra, Levitra, and Cialis. How about stop playing with your privates and give us something for cancer!
—Unknown

A little humor here to bring a smile to you face today! For humor is a very good medicine that you need daily!

DAY 223

Friendship improves our happiness, and abates misery, by doubling our joy and dividing our grief.
—Joseph Addison, 1672-1719
English Poet

Ah, yes! The magic of friendship, happiness, and joy. Your team, your friends that you have encircled around you for this journey will help provide that happiness you need. They will help keep misery from knocking at your front door by bringing you joy and more. They will help with your grief by giving you a shoulder to cry and an ear to listen to you. True friends are with you through thick and thin. They don't run and hide when your going gets tough. They are there for you to help with the battle. They carry magic powers for you, just like the good wizard! Keep them close!

DAY 224

When written in Chinese, the word "crisis" is composed of two characters—one represents danger, the other represents opportunity.
—John F. Kennedy, 1917-1963
35th President of the United States

You have your crisis going on right now. Yes, it presents you with great danger. It is a battle of life and death. Remember that second Chinese character for the "crisis": opportunity. You are presented the opportunity to stand up and battle this crisis of yours. You have the opportunity to be brave and strong. To show your great courage. To have great faith and hope. To be resolute. To be victorious. These are all opportunities. You and you alone decide if you will take advantage of this opportunity and fight on. Take the opportunity each day! Fight on! Be the champion that you are!

DAY 225

Two men look out through the same bars; one sees the mud, the other the stars.
　　　　　—Frederick Langbridge, 1849-1922
　　　　　　　　British Chaplain

Two men, cancer patients, look out through the hospital window; one sees the mud from the storm, the other sees the rainbow from the storm. Who lives longer?

DAY 226

A cheerful face is nearly as good for an invalid as healthy weather.
　　　　　—Benjamin Franklin, 1706-1790
　　A Founding Father of the United States

A cheerful face is nearly as good for a cancer patient as healthy weather. Cheerfulness is your friend. It can make almost any difficult situation bearable. Cheerfulness is one of those weapons against cancer. Use it as much as you can. It never runs out of ammo. It is not just receiving cheerfulness; you must give it as well. When you do so, that cheerfulness you give comes back and shines on you. It's not like it is hard to spread cheerfulness.

It is pretty damn easy to do. A simple smile can work. Simple kind words will work. My favorite, cracking a joke, will work. Well, if it is a good joke. Offering positive thoughts will work. Try it; you will be amazed at the cheerfulness you can produce in others that come right back to you. Next time you're at the grocery store, smile at other shoppers and say hello. Be ready to catch some cheerfulness coming back at you.

You're not in a cheerful situation but being cheerful will help you so much!

DAY 227

What is defeat? Nothing but education, nothing but the first steps to something better.
—Wendell Phillips, 1811-1884
American Advocate

If you are like me, you dislike the word *defeat* with a passion. Defeat should be replaced with opportunity. Because that is exactly what it is. Like Mr. Phillips said, "the first steps to something better." The opportunity to come at it another day. It is an education if you learn from it and go back at it. You will have moments throughout the journey that are "defeats", i.e. opportunities. Learn from them. Do not get discouraged. Remember they are steps to a better you, to a better place!

DAY 228

Life is a like a game of tables; the chances are not in our power, but the playing is.
—Terence McKenna, 1946-2000
American Author

Your cancer is your game of tables. The chances are not in your power, but the playing is. How will you play the remainder of your game? Play it with confidence. Play it with faith and hope. Play it with determination. Play it with courage. Play it to win!

DAY 229

I am more convinced that our happiness or unhappiness depends far more on the way we meet the events of life than on the nature of those events themselves.
—Wilhelm Von Humboldt, 1767-1835
Prussian Philosopher

Happiness, happiness, and more happiness; so important you get to read about throughout this book. When you receive your diagnosis, there is of course the initial unhappiness. The nature of your event is what brings you the unhappiness. How you meet the journey is the key. Be happy with the plan of attack your physicians have laid out for you. Your buy in to this gives you the happiness to fuel the journey. This is also of the same importance if you have to restart at some point of your journey because of changes in your condition. Meet all these challenges positively along this journey and let happiness help you.

DAY 230

Nothing is so contagious as enthusiasm. It is the real allegory of the tale of Orpheus; it moves stones and charms brutes. It is the genius of sincerity and truth accomplishes no victories without it.
—Edward Bulwer-Lytton, 1803-1873
English Poet

If enthusiasm can move stones for Orpheus, what can it do for you? If it can charm brutes for Orpheus, what can it do for you? I would say, "Sign me up for some of that enthusiasm!" The Cambridge English Dictionary tells us that enthusiasm is *a feeling of energetic interest in a particular subject or activity.*

Whether you call it enthusiasm or fervor or passion or zeal or keenness or vigor, it is that something you want to have throughout a battle with cancer. When you have it and show it, your team sees it and catches it. Giving you a double dose of it. Cancer is your stone and your brute. Let your enthusiasm charm your cancer and then move it aside. Be enthused to make your journey successful!

DAY 231

He who fears he will suffer, already suffers because of his fear.
—Michel Eyquem De Montaigne, 1533-1592
                              French Author

You had your initial fear when you found out about your cancer. Then your physicians laid out your plan for this journey. That fear subsided and you gained some confidence and the desire to get to work on that plan. Fear will show up at different times throughout your journey. Remember, with fear comes courage. Let the courage wash the fear away so you can keep pushing. Letting your fear bring you the courage necessary, so that fear doesn't eat you up and hold you back from the task at hand.

DAY 232

We can't help everyone, but everyone can help someone.
　　　　　　　—Ronald Reagan, 1911-2004
　　　　　　40th President of the United States

Everyone can help someone! That is what your team signed up for, to help you through this journey. That can't help everyone, but they sure can help you. They can help you in so many ways: show you compassion, bring you love, show unbridled enthusiasm, share time with you, encourage you, offer their shoulder for you to cry on, give you positive reinforcement, help keep you focused, and so on and so on. Allow them to help someone; allow them to help you!

DAY 233

What counts is not necessarily the size of the dog in the fight—it's the size of the fight in the dog.
　　　　—Dwight D. Eisenhower, 1890-1969
　　　　34th President of the United States

What is the size of fight in you? Think large, think really large. This is a long journey that is not easy.

You need to keep your fight fed. Make sure it gets plenty of the essentials it needs: faith, hope, determination, positivity, love, vigor, stamina, and enthusiasm. You may not be the biggest dog on the block, but you have the biggest fight and the best bite. Go take a bite out of cancer!

DAY 234

Just because you're down to your last strike, you're not out yet. You can always do more. You'll always have more at bats to take. That's true in baseball and in life generally.
—Tony LaRussa, 1944-present
American Professional Baseball Mgr.

Don't ever give up! There is always hope. Just look to Tony's 2011 St. Louis Cardinal team. Late in the regular season that team was 10 ½ games out of the playoffs. On the very last day of the season, they clinched the last spot for the playoffs. They rode that momentum through the playoffs and on to the World Series. Forward to Game 6 in St. Louis, the Texas Rangers led the Series three games to two. The Rangers took a 7-4 lead into the eighth inning. Then Tony's team put his quotation to practice. The Cardinals scored one run in the eighth. Then down to their last strike in the bottom of the ninth, they scored two more runs to tie the game. Then in the bottom of the tenth, after Texas scored two in the top of the inning, they were down to their last strike again. Yes, that's right, they scored two more runs to tie the game again. Then in the bottom of the eleventh inning, David Freese hit one of the most historic home runs in World Series history and sent the World Series to a seventh game. As ESPN senior sports writer Gene Wojciechowski said in his article about the game: *"eleven wonderfully bizarre, deliciously dramatic innings".* Many sport journalists immediately calling this game one of the greatest games ever. Something you will tell your kids about. The Cardinals went on to win their 11th World Series Championship.

You may feel several times during your journey that you are down to your last strike. That is not time to throw in the towel. It's time to get ready for the next pitch. You can do more. You'll always have more at bats. It's not over 'til the fat lady sings, right? Well, the fat lady didn't sing in St. Louis that night and we are not going to let her sing to you, either. Get yourself ready for the pitch!

DAY 235

Virtually nothing in impossible in this world if you just put your mind to it and maintain a positive attitude.
—Lou Holtz, 1937-present
American College & NFL Coach

Solid words from a solid coach. Lou Holtz instilled this into his players. Especially his 1988 Notre Dame Fighting Irish. That team went undefeated that year and went on to win the National Championship. They beat teams that end the season ranked #2, #4, #5 and #7. The won 10 out of their 12 games by double digits. That team is considered the best undefeated team in the history of college football. Nothing is impossible when you have a positive attitude about it!

You can use this philosophy when battling cancer. Maintain your positive attitude throughout the journey. Rely on your team to keep you positive and energized. Keep your mind on the prize. Don't be distracted by things outside of the battle. This cannot be done alone and you have a great team around, just like Lou Holtz had with his 1988 Fighting Irish. Play your way to the championship!

DAY 236

In every battle there comes a time when both sides consider themselves beaten, then he who continues the attacks wins.
—Ulysses S. Grant, 1822-1885
18th President of the United States

Ulysses became famous as a Union General in the Civil War. He was highly respected by President Lincoln for his willingness to fight. General Grant used the philosophy above to secure major victories at the battle of Belmont, Fort Henry, and Fort Donelson. These were tough battles with many losses on each side. Grant pushed through with attacks and won, earning him great popularity that he used to win the Presidency of the United States.

Read that a second time. When you feel beaten, continue the attack! You have what it takes for victory. You have all the tools necessary for victory. You have assembled a great team for this battle. You have a great plan for the battle from your physicians. You are prepared! Just have to keep pushing. Keep pushing through the hard days. Don't hesitate. Don't stop. Give it your best! We are here with you!

DAY 237

You have to motivate yourself with challenges. That's how you know you're still alive.
—Jerry Seinfeld, 1954-present
American Comedian & Actor

You have one of the biggest challenges in life: battling cancer. You should feel motivated each and every day by this challenge. You know you are alive each morning when you rise to face the cancer. You and your team need to keep you motivated throughout this journey. That motivation is the will to live. You may not beat cancer, but when you stay motivated and give it your best, your legacy will live on. Which in the end does mean you were victorious!

DAY 238

Courage is being scared to death and saddling up anyway.
—John Wayne, 1907-1979
American Actor

Who would ever think that John Wayne was ever scared? Well, the Duke fought the battle you are fighting now twice. He knows of what he speaks. He was diagnosed with lung cancer in 1964 and had his left lung removed. He made it through that first battle by doing just as he said, saddling up anyway. In 1979 cancer paid him a second visit, this time in his stomach. The Duke once again saddled up for the fight. Showing he still had a ton of courage. Cancer did get the best of him on June 11, 1979. I remember as a child thinking John Wayne was one of the toughest men in the world. You know what—after learning his biography, he was. He saddled up twice to cancer.

You have saddled up already the day you started this journey. You are out there riding with The Duke! The key now is to stay in that saddle and ride to journey's end. Your courage has gotten you this far; let it get you the rest of the way.

DAY 239

You have to feel confident. If you don't, then you're going to be hesitant and defensive, and there'll be a lot of things working against you.
—Clint Eastwood, 1930-present
American Actor

Alwaysgreater.com gives us some very good reasons to be confident:

1. Freedom from self-doubt: the more confident you become, the more free you become of the mental torture of doubting yourself.
2. Greater strength and capabilities: the more confident you are, the stronger and more powerful you feel.
3. Freedom from fear and anxiety: the confident you become, the more you know that you can accept, handle, learn, gain, and benefit from any situation, circumstance, or outcome.
4. More energy and motivation to act: the more confident you are that you can achieve things you want to achieve, the more motivated and energized you are to take action to achieve them.

Pretty good reasons to be confident in your journey. You can not hesitate or be defensive. That is when you give cancer the opportunity the strike more and strike harder. Your confidence can may keep that at bay. Cancer does not need any opportunities. You need all those opportunities. Stay confident!

DAY 240

I believe that if life gives you lemons, you should make lemonade... and try to find somebody whose life has given them vodka and have a party.

—Ron White, 1956-present
American Comedian

You have been given a bunch of lemons with your cancer and need to make some lemonade. Now find the person on your team that life has given vodka to. Mix the two together and relax with a team party. Relaxation is part of your daily plan from the physicians.

Your humor for the day!

DAY 241

I think it's important to find the little things in everyday life that make you happy.

—Paula Cole, 1968-present
American Singer-Songwriter

As you already know, happiness is very important for you during this difficult and long journey. You need to find all those little things that make you happy and let them give you energy. Let them keep your flame burning. The littlest of things will work: a butterfly that lands on your arm, a smile from the mailman, your flowers blooming in the garden, the beauty of a full moon, the smell of a summer's morning, your radio station plays your favorite song, your favorite team wins their game, a baby bunny plays in your backyard. So many everyday little things can bring you happiness. Don't overlook them!

DAY 242

The good physician treats the disease; the great physician treats the patient who has the disease.
—William Osler, 1849-1919
Co-founder of John Hopkins Hospital

Hopefully your oncologist is a great physician! With this hideous disease, all oncologists need to be. We know that is not the case, though. It is just as important to treat you as it is to treat the cancer itself. If the oncologist doesn't have you in mind with his or her treatment plan, there is a problem. Part of that plan needs to be keeping you confident, determined, positive, strong, and hopeful. It is not just about jacking you up with a bunch of chemotherapy and/or radiation. You do have a heart and soul under that skin of yours. And they need to be attended to as well.

DAY 243

To array a man's will against his sickness is the supreme art of medicine.
　　　　　—Henry Ward Beecher, 1813-1887
　　　　　American Congregationalist Clergyman

This is where your team can really help. Keeping your will lined up against your cancer. Your willpower will be put to a test on this journey. Allow your team to keep that will pumped up and ready to go. When you lose that will, you lost the battle and when you lose this battle, we lose you. Let your team of family, friends, loved ones, caretakers, and physicians find that special spot, the supreme art of medicine.

DAY 244

You never want to have that ticking clock and know that you had all this time and didn't use it.
　　　　　—J.J. Abrams, 1966-present
　　　　　American Film Director

You need to keep outrunning that ticking clock. Don't hesitate, don't stop. Keep pushing ahead on your journey. You do not want to give cancer the chance of catching up to you. Keep it in your rearview mirror.

Don't get distracted and end up wasting time, either. The last thing you want is for the end to come sooner than you thought and you left a bunch of time on the table. Maximize every minute you have!

DAY 245

Comedy can be a cathartic way to deal with personal trauma.
—Robin Williams, 1951-2014
American Comedian

Robin knew this very well. He had Lewy body dementia and used his comedy to help deal with it. It worked very well for him for many years. Many people close to Robin did not know he was struggling with this disease. When he died on August 11, 2014, people all over the world were shocked to hear about his death and his disease. He was a great comedian!

Let comedy be a cathartic way to deal with your cancer. Try to keep some humor and laughter in your daily routine. Robin's movie, *Mrs. Doubtfire*, would be a good one to watch to get some comedy relief. That movie simply cracks me up. I'm not one to laugh out loud while watching a show or movie, but I can't help myself with this one. You can also watch the old *Mork & Mindy* Shows. Robin was classic in those programs as well. Silly show, but great comedy. You need to find time each day laugh!

DAY 246

One must not let oneself be overwhelmed by sadness.
　　　　　　　—Jackie Kennedy, 1929-1994
　　　　Former First Lady of the United States

Mrs. Kennedy knew all too well about sadness. As First Lady of the United States on November 22, 1963, she was riding in a motorcade with her husband, President John F. Kennedy, when he was assassinated in Dallas, Texas. Our whole nation was overwhelmed by sadness that weekend. Ask someone that lived through that and they can tell you exactly where they were when they heard the news. How could Mrs. Kennedy not be overwhelmed by this? I think it is safe to say, at first, she was overwhelmed. With help and support from Robert Kennedy, the President's brother, and the Kennedy family she was able to not be overwhelmed by the President's death in the days ahead and was a very strong presence for her children.

Do not find yourself overwhelmed by sadness that cancer can bring. If you start feeling that way, that is the time to call on someone from your team.

Have them come visit you. Have a good conversation. Cry on their shoulder if you need to. Share a laugh and a smile. You will snap out of that overwhelmed feeling before they leave. Jackie had Robert and the other Kennedys. You have a solid team.

DAY 247

My attitude has always been, if you fall flat on your face, at least you're moving forward. All you have to do is get back up and try again.
—Richard Branson, 1950-present
English Business Magnate

Mr. Branson has fallen on his face more than once along the way to becoming one of the greatest business men of our time. He dropped out of school at the age of 16 to start his first business venture. That start in business led him to found Virgin Group. The Virgin Group is made up of over 400 companies. When a business venture failed and he had fallen face first, he just got back up and continued to move ahead. He practices what he preaches and he is very successful at that. In 2000 the Queen of England knighted him. In 2002 the BBC listed him on the list of the 100 greatest Britons. *Forbes* Magazine listed his net worth at $5.1 billion in 2017. He is very successful.

You will encounter times along this journey when you fall. Try to fall face first like Mr. Branson, so that you still are moving forward when falling. Then get back up and continue your progress down your journey's path. With any luck, maybe you can be 1/10th as successful as Mr. Branson. Which is still pretty darn good!

DAY 248

Just scream! You vent, and the body just feels good after a good old yell.
   —Carol Burnett, 1933-present
   American Comedian & Actress

Is that why Carol screamed like Tarzan on her show? When I was still in the retail grocery industry directing a store, I sometimes would go out the back door and give a good yell to the open field behind my store. It always made me feel much better. I was able to come back to my office and calmly handle the situation that made me scream. It is a good feeling sometimes to release some anger, tension, and anxiety. All three of which you do not want to have built up in you while on a long journey with cancer. So, go ahead and give it a try. Maybe even try to do it the Carol Burnett way, like Tarzan, to give you a good laugh at the same time; two birds, one stone.

DAY 249

I love those who can smile in trouble, who can gather strength from distress, and grow brave reflection.
—Leonardo Da Vinci, 1452-1519
Italian Renaissance Polymath

We love those people as well! Hopefully Leonardo was describing you and how you are handling your cancer battle. You have a smile on your face each day when you bring laughter to your journey. You get your daily strength and courage from the fear cancer brings. You show your bravery each day this journey continues. This seems to be a pretty good formula for a successful journey!

DAY 250

Satisfaction lies in the effort, not in the attainment; full effort is full victory.
—Mahatma Gandhi, 1869-1948
Indian Activist

Give it your best effort all the way through. That full effort will give you a full victory regardless of the final outcome. Be at peace with that. I know both Jim and Julie were at peace with this exact quote.

They gave the total effort right to the end. They both attained victory. Their legacy and their memory with live with us forever.

DAY 251

When you have to cope with a lot of problems, you're either going to sink or you're going to swim.
—Tom Cruise, 1962-present
American Actor

Cancer is a problem; no doubt about that! It brings you a lot of problems. You are coping with these problems each day. You have already been swimming to keep yourself from sinking under this cancer. Treat this like the Olympic 4X200M relay. Get your team involved to help you keep swimming. They're there and they're there for you; use them! Bring home the gold medal!

DAY 252

A mind concerned about danger is a clouded mind. It's paralyzing.
—Buzz Aldrin, 1930-present
American Astronaut

Ronald J. Avery

Buzz know all about danger. He flew F-86 Sabres in the Korean War and battled with MiG-15s. That is danger. He was the pilot for Gemini 12, the last Gemini mission. He set a record on the mission with a five-hour spacewalk. That is danger. Buzz then moved on to the Apollo program and made the first lunar landing with Neil Armstrong on July 20, 1969. He then became the second man to walk on the moon on July 21, 1969. That is danger. At age 86 he ventured to the South Pole, becoming the oldest person to do so. That is danger. Buzz never let danger cloud his mind or paralyze him. Danger is something that can be overcome.

Do not let your concern for danger that cancer brings you cloud your mind and paralyze your journey. Keep your mind free for positive thoughts of faith, hope, courage, and love. Danger is only danger if you allow it to be.

DAY 253

The most exhausting thing in life is to be insincere.
—Anne Morrow Lindbergh, 1906-2001
American Aviator & Author

Is there any reason on God's green earth for anyone to be insincere? No, there is not! Do not allow a person like that into your inner circle or onto your team. People like that are another type of cancer you do not need to waste time and space on. An insincere person is almost always very visible in a crowd. They are the person everyone else is looking at with strange looks on their face. Like, "What the heck?!" You can usually hear them before you see them also with their loud lines of crap. When you hear them or see them, walk away. Walk away as fast as you can. Don't look at them, just get out of there!

DAY 254

Prayer is man's greatest power!
—W. Clement Stone, 1902-2002
American Businessman

Use this power once to twice daily as needed. This is a strong medication for you. It will clear your mind of any negative thoughts and allow for all the good vibes to enter into your heart and soul. The power of prayer should not be underestimated. James 5:16-18 states: "The prayer of a righteous man is powerful and effective. Elijah was a man just like us. He prayed earnestly that it would not rain, and it did not rain on the land for three and half years. Again, he prayed, and the heavens gave rain, and the earth produce its crops." In Matthew

Ronald J. Avery

17:20 Jesus taught: "I tell you the truth, if you have faith as small as a mustard seed, you can say to this mountain 'Move from here to there' and it will move. Nothing will be impossible for you."

God's help through the power of prayer is available to all of us. You do not to recite words from a book. Speak to God through your heart and soul. God will listen to your request and your issues. Do this in thanksgiving of him and his son Jesus Christ. Use this power freely to ease all your anxiety.

DAY 255

If the world seems cold to you, kindle fires to warm it.
—Lucy Larcom, 1824-1893
American Poet

When your world, spirit, starts to feel cold from the long journey you are on, kindle those fires within by calling upon your faith, bravery, courage, determination, hope, and love. Let those fires grow and bring you the warmth to your world needed to continue on your journey. Keep plenty of kindling on hand, so your flames don't go low and make your spirit cold. Make sure it is that good kindling that consist of faith, bravery, courage, determination, hope, and love. This kindling brings great warmth!

DAY 256

What we achieve inwardly will change outer reality.
—Plutarch, 46 AD-120 AD
Greek Biographer

You know by now what you need to achieve inwardly to help you and aid you on your journey. Make sure you keep achieving these. All those that were mentioned in yesterday's message: faith, bravery, courage, determination, hope, and love. You can add a positive mental state, inner strength, optimism, persistence, vigor, and acceptance. All the above can help change your reality with cancer. Possibly making your cancer a footnote of your past.

DAY 257

I believe that everything you work at and want in life is a great challenge.
—Anthony Rizzo, 1989-present
American Professional Baseball Player

Anthony knows this all too well. An **MLB.com** article titled *Rizzo's Triumph Over Cancer* tells us a little bit about his story with Hodgkin's lymphoma.

While playing in the minor for the Boston Red Sox in 2007, Anthony was diagnosed with Hodgkin's lymphoma at the age of 18. He was brought to Boston by the team to talk with Red Sox pitcher Jon Lester who himself battled lymphoma. Lester spoke to Rizzo about the many challenges of battling cancer. Also, the positive attitude required to attack it. In 2008 Rizzo began six months of chemotherapy. In September of that year all the tumors where gone and he was in full remission.

The rest of Anthony Rizzo's story is all icing on the cake for him. Rizzo ended up going to play for the Chicago Cubs and has become one of the best first basemen in baseball today. He has been on the All-Star team, his team has won their divisional championship, his team has won their league's championship and most of all, his Cubs won a World Series for the first time in over 100 years. Rizzo's life in remission has been magical. Rizzo is beloved by his teammates, by the city of Chicago and by baseball fans on many teams. He is simply a class act and someone every kid playing Little League Baseball can look up to with great pride.

You have life's greatest challenge: cancer. You are working at this challenge. You want to put your cancer in remission just like Rizzo. You can do that if you stay on your course with a positive attitude and hopes of better tomorrows.

DAY 258

For me life is continuously being hungry. The meaning of life is not simply to exist, to survive, but to move ahead, to go up, to achieve, to conquer.
—Arnold Schwarzenegger, 1947-present
Austrian-American Actor

Arnold is one who practices what he preaches. The storyline of his life is exactly what is stated above in his quote. At the age of 15 he started weight training. By the time he was 20 he had won the Mr. Universe title and went on to win seven Mr. Olympia titles. I would say he was hungry. He moved ahead, went up to achieve and to conquer! He wasn't done there. He went on to Hollywood and became an action film icon with movies like *Conan the Barbarian, The Terminator,* and *Total Recall,* to name a few. Again, showing his hunger for life and to conquer. He wasn't done here, either. In 2003 he was elected to be the 38th Governor of California and served two terms. He earned himself the great nickname, *Governator.* After leaving office in 2011, he went back to acting. He still remains hungry for life, looking to achieve and conquer. When Arnold says, "I'll be back," he really means it!

For you right now in your situation, need to be hungry for a healthy and cancer-free you. You need to move ahead, to go up the path to cancer freedom and conquer this hideous disease. If you just simply exist, cancer will be the one conquering!

DAY 259

Caring—about people, about things, about life—is an act of maturity.
—Tracy McMillan, 1964-present
American Author

Don't stop caring! Be as mature as you possibly can. Care for the people you have around you who are caring for you during this journey. Care that this journey is of utmost importance for you. Care about your life and what it means to yourself, to family, to your loved ones, and to your friends. Let all that caring burn into energy for you to continue your journey. Let it fuel your hopes and dreams. Let it give you faith in this journey and faith in your God. Let it give you great determination and persistence against your cancer. Let it bring you happiness!

DAY 260

Hitch your wagon to a star.
—Ralph Waldo Emerson, 1803-1882
American Poet

Hitch your wagon, loaded with your hopes and dreams, to a star and let it carry you to journey's end and the beginning of the new you. The new, healthy you that is free from cancer and ready to start the next chapter of your life. Let that next chapter be filled with an abundance of happiness and joy!

DAY 261

Set your sights high, the higher the better. Expect the most wonderful things to happen, not in the future, but right now. Realize that nothing is too good. Allow absolutely nothing to hamper you or hold you up in any way.
—Eileen Caddy, 1917-2006
Scottish Author

You really do need to set your sights high for this journey. Don't be satisfied with anything but high expectations. The results of this journey are of life and death. Your sights need to be of the former, not the latter. Your sights need to be on all your hopes and dreams that this journey will be successful. Do not be distracted, do not slow down; keep pushing forward with your sights set high!

DAY 262

I come to win.
—Leo Durocher, 1905-1991
American Professional Baseball Player

Leo did come to win every day as a player and manager in Major League Baseball. He did have a large ego, which got him in trouble throughout his career. That ego and the attitude of winning did lead him to many great accomplishments. As a player he was on two World Series Championship teams, the 1928 Yankees and the 1934 Cardinals. He also won two more as a manager. When he retired from baseball, he ranked fifth with managerial wins in 2009. Leo did come to win.

You need to tell yourself "I come to win" each morning when you're looking in the mirror. Keep your confidence high. Try to win each day. Hopefully it will lead you to a championship!

DAY 263

Things are never quite as scary when you've got a best friend.
—Bill Watterson, 1958-present
American Cartoonist

Bill brought that to life in his comic strip, *Calvin & Hobbes*. Calvin had his best friend in Hobbes, a life-size stuffed tiger. Calvin was always on some sort of mischievous adventure and had Hobbes with him all the time. I'm sure making it a little less scary.

Your best friend will be there with you on your scary journey. They may be right with you or just a phone call away. If your best friend isn't available, you have the rest of your team to lean on. You will always have someone. No need to be scared. Somebody will always be there to catch you!

DAY 264

In times of great stress or adversity, it's always best to keep busy, to plow your anger and your energy into something positive.
—Lee Iacocca, 1924-current
American Automotive Executive

Mr. Iacocca has battled great stress and adversity in his automotive career. He took over control of the Chrysler Corporation in 1978. The company at that time was on life support. By the time he left Chrysler in 1992, he brought the company back to life. He plowed all his anger and energy into the company. He became the face of Chrysler. I remember him doing all the commercials for the company in the 1980s. He turned Chrysler into something positive, alright.

You are dealing with great stress and adversity right now. Keep yourself busy. Take the energy of the anger from cancer and turn it into something positive each day. Let your energy bring you small victories day by day. Those small positives may turn into one big positive for you at the end of your journey. Harness your energy!

DAY 265

"Impossible" is a word only to be found in the dictionary of fools.
—Napoleon Bonaparte, 1808-1873
French Emperor

You could remove Napoleon's name from this quote and insert James D. Avery. The word *impossible* was never in Jim's dictionary, either. Jim would always find a way to figure things out. When he was running his Avery Railing Company in the Millwork District of Dubuque, neighbors from other companies would always come over to Jim's shop when they had a problem they could not solve. He would figure it out for them. People thought some of his inventions were impossible. Well, they were not and he brought them to life. The most famous was his Avery Dicycle, which won an International Engineering Award. He also invented another bike called "The Chemo Bike". Which, by the name, he developed while going through chemotherapy treatments. He had several other inventions he made. The word *impossible* to Jim meant he was going to figure it out.

Don't allow this word in your personal dictionary. Think about it like Jim thought about it. If you have a bad diagnosis of cancer, stage 3 or 4, it's not impossible. Work hard, give the effort, and you are successful. You will be our hero.

DAY 266

If you want to conquer fear, don't think about yourself. Try to help others and your fears will vanish.

—Dale Carnegie, 1888-1955
American Writer & Lecturer

Julie was the Queen of this quote. She never thought of herself during her journey with cancer. It was always about helping us understand the disease and what it was doing to her and that everything would be okay, no matter the final outcome. She eased our fears while conquering her own. I remember being so proud of the way she handled herself. Well, I'm still very proud today! She helped this young man understand life, the full circle of life. She was a Queen that became a beautiful Angel, a guardian Angel for me and my family.

As you are going through your journey, you will have times of fear. Don't dwell on that fear. Think about how you can help others within your circle. Then act on that. Don't let them be distracted with the fear of losing you. When that happens, they won't be much help for you. If everyone helps everyone, fear should not negatively affect your journey.

DAY 267

If wrinkles must be written upon your brows, let them not be written upon the heart. The spirit should not grow old.
        —James Garfield, 1831-1881
        20th President of the United Sates

365 Days for Hope

You may have wrinkles of pain and suffering upon your brow from the cancer you battle. The key is not to let those wrinkles fall upon your heart and soul. Your heart and soul deliver the energy you need each day to battle cancer. We must keep them wrinkle-free from any pain and suffering. As long as you keep your faith, hope, and courage, they will be protected from this. Maintain your courage so that you will have continuous faith and hope during this battle.

DAY 268

> *It is not how much we have, but how much we enjoy, that makes happiness.*
> —Charles H. Spurgeon, 1834-1892
> English Baptist Preacher

A cancer patient given a terminal diagnosis that has little but enjoys every minute of the time he has left knows of happiness. The one with plenty that complains "why me" will not know of happiness before he passes. I think I would choose little and enjoy my time, so I understood happiness before I left this good earth. What about you?

Jim and Julie both understood this before they passed. Neither had plenty, but both took advantage of every minute before they passed to find enjoyment. They knew of true happiness upon their death. They found that true happiness all during their last days with us.

DAY 269

When a man dies, if he can pass enthusiasm along to his children, he has left them an estate of incalculable value.
     —Thomas Edison, 1847-1931
     American Inventor

Jim did not have any children, but he did pass on his enthusiasm to many: his family, his friends, the National Mississippi River Museum, the children at the Workers Space, bike enthusiasts and people of the Dubuque Millwork District. His estate was beyond riches and touched many. Many more than he would have ever thought. He is legendary and has touched many.

Do everything with enthusiasm along this journey. Let that enthusiasm trickle down to your family, friends, and loved ones. If you pass away from this hideous disease, you, too will leave an estate of incalculable value. You will be legendary. Your legacy written in stone. Have enthusiasm and pass it on!

DAY 270

True peace of mind comes from accepting the worst. Psychologically I think, it means a release of energy.
—Lin Yutang, 1895-1976
Chinese Writer & Inventor

You may have to accept the worst because of your cancer. When you can accept that, you will have true peace of mind. You will feel a release of all the negative energy associated with cancer. We hope you never have to accept the worst. Jim and Julie both faced that worst-case scenario. They accepted their fate and let true peace settle with in them. It was then that they were able to help us, the family members wrap our heads around their fate. This takes true courage; it takes a hero. If you end up facing this, hopefully you have the courage to accept and then to help your loved ones. You will be their hero!

DAY 271

There is a destiny that makes us brothers; none goes his way alone; all that we send into the lives of others comes back into our own.
—Edwin Markham, 1852-1940
American Poet

Ronald J. Avery

None goes his way alone. You are not alone on this journey. You have assembled your brothers, team, to assist you during this long difficult journey. Send into their lives love, faith, encouragement, and happiness. It shall come back into your own twofold. It is destiny that has brought you all together on this journey. Now you can work together to determine your future destiny!

DAY 272

The truth is that life is delicious, charming, frightful, sweet, bitter and that it is everything.
—Anatole France, 1844-1924
French Poet

Life always comes full circle. Traveling many roads, good and bad. Taking you up and then back down. Some days full of love and some days full of dislike. Some days filled with happiness and some with sadness. It is not for us to figure out. Just put your seatbelt on and enjoy the ride. For it will come full circle.

DAY 273

To hear always, to think always, to learn always, it is this that we live truly; he who

aspires to nothing, and learns nothing, is not worthy of living.
—Sir Arthur Helps, 1813-1875
English Writer

Are you truly living? Are you hearing what is around you? Are you thinking always? Most of all, are you learning? Don't stop these activities because of your current journey. Continue them because of your journey! Jim is a very good example of this. He was constantly thinking of new and better ways. He was always learning about the newest and greatest. He always kept his ear to ground, so he wouldn't miss something of importance. He truly lived every day. Don't miss your opportunity to do the same. As Sir Helps states: he who aspires to nothing and learns nothing is not worthy of living. Live to the fullest while you can. Keep hearing, keep thinking, and keep learning!

DAY 274

I cannot know where you are going, but I hold the lamp of my love aloft to accompany you on your way.
—Rabindranath Tagore, 1861-1941
Bengali Poet

If your cancer journey is coming to a close with the ending you hoped would not happen, make peace with yourself and your God. Hopefully you will be able to find time for family. You can let them know all will be okay. They can let you know that it is okay to go. That their love for you will shine brightly so you will find your way. For they do not know where you are going, but their love will be with you always. I was so lucky to have that moment with Jim just a few hours before he passed. I knew he had my lamp of love to take with him when he tried to say my name and nothing came out. I told him, "Go, go be at peace. Take all our love with you." Make it a point to spend some time with your loved ones before you go. It will make everyone at peace.

DAY 275

Be humble in your confidence, yet courageous in your character.
—Melanie Koulouris
American Writer & Lecturer

Jackie Kennedy lived this quote throughout her life. First as the First Lady of the United States when her husband, John F. Kennedy, was sworn in as President on January 20, 1961. She remained very humble in her confidence as she changed the way we looked at the office of the First Lady. Then she showed us how courageous in character she was when President Kennedy was assassinated. She remained that way after her life in the spotlight of Washington D.C. She was humble in that life as a book editor in New York City. She showed her courage for us one more time when she battled Non-Hodgkin's Lymphoma. The lymphoma eventually took her life on May 19, 1994.

Be humble in your confidence that you can complete this journey with success, but let your character shine with courage! You can do this! Just do your thing day in and day out. Quietly going about the business at hand.

DAY 276

True friendship is a plant of slow growth and must undergo and withstand the shocks of adversity before it is entitled to the appellation.
—George Washington, 1732-1799
1st President of the United States

We all have friends come and go, but it is the true friends that we always circle back to. Especially in times of joy and times of grief. Those are the friends that are always there for you. A true friend does not run when the going gets tough. They roll up their sleeves and jump right in there with you. A true friend is someone you see on a regular basis, not just at your birthday party when there is free food and drink. A true friend has your back 24/7. Being a true friend is not a part-time job. Hopefully you have some true friends on your team. If you don't, you better recruit some, asap! Those are the type of people you need at your side on this journey.

DAY 277

I have loved the stars too fondly to be fearful of the night.
—Galileo Galilei, 1564-1642
Italian Polymath

Let's rephrase this for you and your situation. "I have loved life too fondly to be fearful of cancer." Continue to love life very fondly. Work hard and with determination that your life has many more years left in it. If you feel some fear, it is okay. You just turn that fear into courage, right? Harness that love of life you have to give you the strength needed for the journey. To give you the confidence you need. To give you hope of better tomorrows. To strengthen your faith in possibilities.

You love life too fondly to be fearful of cancer! Don't ever give up on your love of life!

DAY 278

A hero is an ordinary individual who finds the strength to persevere and endure in spite of overwhelming obstacles.
—Christopher Reeve, 1952-2004
American Actor

Which makes all cancer patients heroes! You were just an ordinary person 'til cancer brought havoc into your life. You have found the strength to preserve and endure, in spite of the overwhelming obstacle of cancer. You have made it this far in your journey and will make it the rest of the way. You are a hero! Mr. Reeve preserved and endured through his misfortune of becoming a quadriplegic. He was able to accomplish so much after his accident. He was, is, and will always be a Superman to me. Jim will always be my Evel Knievel. Julie will always be my Wonder Woman. Who will you be? Batman? Cat Woman? The Flash? Be our hero today! Persevere and endure in spite of your cancer!

DAY 279

I believe in hope. I believe in believing. Believing that there is a light through all this darkness.
—Lynne Knowlton
Canadian Blogger

Lynne is a cancer survivor. She found her light through her darkest hours. There is light there for all of us to find. Sometimes it takes a long time to find the light. Sometimes you have to work real hard to find the light. Sometimes the light is right there, but we are blinded by distractions and don't see it. Believe in hope! Believe in believing! It is then that you can start to see the light!

DAY 280

Cancer lost the battle against you because it originally planned to make you weaker, but inadvertently made you stronger. Now that you survived, thank the disease for helping you discover the fighter within.
—Unknown

Cancer's plan is to make you weaker, so it can spread throughout your body and take complete control of you. If you stick to your plan, if you allow your team to help, and if you don't lose your faith, hope, confidence, and will to live, the cancer will make you stronger. And we hope, strong enough to complete the journey and win your battle. There is a fighter within you. You just need to bring it forth.

DAY 281

When you come to the end of the rope, tie a knot and hang on.
—Franklin D. Roosevelt, 1882-1945
32nd President of the United States

FDR tied a knot and hung on in 1921 when he contracted a paralytic illness, leaving his legs permanently paralyzed. He did not allow his illness to slow him down or keep him from chasing his dreams. He ran for and won the governorship of New York in 1928. Then in the 1932 presidential election, he ran as a Democrat against Herbert Hoover and won in a landslide. He went on to win four presidential elections and is the only person to win that more than twice. He led the United States out of the Great Depression with landmark legislation. He was president during World War II and worked closely with Winston Churchill of England to defeat Nazi Germany. FDR died while in office during his fourth term. He never let his physical handicap keep him from his dreams. He had a firm grip on the end of his rope.

When you feel you are at the end of the rope with your battle against cancer, do as FDR: tie a knot and hang on. Keep battling; things will get better.

Don't let the cancer keep you from your dreams and ambitions. Never give up and hang on!

DAY 282

There is no education like adversity.
—Benjamin Disraeli, 1804-1881
British Prime Minister

Well then, cancer patients are going to school 24/7. Their education is a personal one. They educate themselves on their own strength, their faith, their hope of better days, their attitude, their determination, their heart, their soul, their courage, their bravery, and more. Adversity gives people an opportunity to get up close and personal with themselves. To learn more about themselves so they can overcome the adversity before them. Keep learning, so you, too can overcome your adversity with cancer.

DAY 283

Always bear in mind that your own resolution to succeed is more important than any other one thing.
—Abraham Lincoln, 1809-1865
16th President of the United States

Lincoln was resolute as president. President Lincoln saved the Union in the Civil War against the Confederates of the south, which then led to the abolition of slavery. President had to stay very resolute during the Civil War. The war was the bloodiest war in United States history. Many lives were lost and many more injured. He kept the war going even after the confederates had the upper hand. After the victory by the Union, Lincoln moved to set all slaves free with the Emancipation Proclamation. It was Lincoln's wish that all men everywhere could be free. Thank God President Lincoln was resolute on victory over the Confederates and that all men could and should be free.

Can you be as resolute as President Lincoln in succeeding over cancer? For you, it is more important than any other thing. Hold firm and keep pushing ever forward. You will face adversity just as the Union Army did. Don't let that erode your resolution for success. You can do this!

DAY 284

Hope is living with courage and confidence, not fear.

—Penny Buldrey
Cancer Survivor

Penny did exactly this during her journey with cancer. She used that philosophy to defeat cancer and become cancer-free. We have used these three words often in this book: hope, courage, and confidence. They are very meaningful words for you and very important to your journey. When you feel fear, you use that to build your courage, which in turn gives you hope and confidence. It is a pretty easy formula. Use it throughout your entire journey and you may have the same results as Penny.

DAY 285

Oh, my friend, it's not what they take away from you that counts... it's what you do with what you have left.
 —Hubert Humphrey, 1911-1978
 38th Vice President of the United States

When Julie was diagnosed with her cancer at the Mayo Clinic in Rochester, Minnesota, the doctors let her and our mother know that the best route to take was to amputate her leg. Julie was very courageous about this and a few days later she had the surgery. She was not going to let that slow her down. They took her leg away, but she did plenty with what she had left. That winter she and I learned to ski. Her with her one leg and me with two. Guess who was better after a few lessons? Correct—Julie! She did not stop with hitting the slopes. She kept going, do everything bigger and better. Oh, my friend, it's not what they took away from Julie that counts... it's what she did with what she had left!

Use what you have to continue your journey, doing what makes you happy along the way. The happiness you get will keep you fueled for the rest of your journey. Try skiing; worked well for Julie!

DAY 286

You only live once, but if you do it right, once is enough.

—Mae West, 1893-1980
American Actress

Mae lived this quotation to its fullest. Her career of seven decades was filled with no regret work and what she felt was right. Jim was very much like Mae. He lived his life right for him, his way with no regrets. Like Mae, he didn't care what any critics might say. He did it his way and he did it amazingly! He told me a few months before he passed that he had no regrets. He did what he wanted to do and accomplished what he wanted to do. He lived his life right for him!

As you are on your journey, don't forget that you need to live. Don't have any regrets! Do it right for you! You only have this one chance, so make it count! Having cancer, you never know when your life will come to a close. Make every minute count.

DAY 287

Strength does not come from physical capacity, it comes from indomitable will.
— Mahatma Gandhi, 1869-1948
Indian Activist

This is very true. We have seen similar thoughts in earlier quotes. Jim and Julie both had that indomitable will that gave them great strength. Their will to fight and to comfort those around them will forever be etched in my mind. When I feel I don't have any physical or mental strength, I think of them and push on. Knowing that they pushed on through a much more difficult situation. The strongest man in the world does not have as much strength as a cancer patient pushing through his or her battle with cancer. Don't lose your faith, hope, or will on this journey. You will need them!

DAY 288

You wouldn't have won if we'd beaten you.
— Yogi Berra, 1925-2015
American Professional Baseball Player

Can't you just hear cancer saying this to a person who beat and survived his or her battle with the evil beast? I'm not sure if he could put such a nice play on words as Yogi, but I'm sure it would be along those same lines. Yogi's quotes can put a smile on most, so smile! It's good for you.

DAY 289

I don't work at being ordinary.
—Paul McCartney, 1942-present
English Singer-Songwriter

These are words you would think came from Jim. His famous line of, "I lead an ordinary life." My brother, I would say you worked like Sir Paul. You didn't work at being ordinary; your time with us was extraordinary!

Don't go through your life as ordinary. Make a statement with your life. Leave a legacy behind for everyone to enjoy. With cancer, you have no idea when your time here is up. Make use of your time now! Work at being extraordinary! Leave your mark on your time here.

DAY 290

It is not my nature, when I see people borne down by the weight of their shackles—the oppression of their tyranny—to make life more bitter by heaping upon them greater burdens; but rather would I do all in my power to raise the yoke than to add anything that would tend to crush them.
—Abraham Lincoln, 1809-1865
16th President of the United States

It is not this Foundation's nature, when we see people borne down by the weight of cancer treatments—the oppression of their tyranny—to make their life more bitter by heaping upon them greater burdens; but rather would we do all in our power to raise the yoke than to add anything that would tend to crush them. We cannot let them stand alone to carry these burdens.

DAY 291

Carry out a random act of kindness, with no expectations of reward, safe in the knowledge that one day someone might do the same for you.
—Princess Diana, 1961-1997
Princess of Wales

365 Days for Hope

Have you carried out a random act of kindness? You should try to do this on a regular basis. Safe in the knowledge that someone might do the same for you. You need all the random acts of kindness onto you as possible when battling your cancer.

Lady Diana carried out so many acts of kindness in her short life: an international campaign to ban landmines, HIV/AIDS work in Africa, work for people with mental illness, and many other charitable works throughout the world. In return she received many, many acts of kindness. She was one of the most loved people in the world.

Carry out acts of kindness! They will return to you and help you on your journey.

DAY 292

Nobody who ever gave his best regretted it.
—George "Papa Bear" Halas, 1895-1983
National Football League Owner & Coach

Papa Bear always gave his best as a captain in the seventh Naval Fleet, as the owner of the Chicago Bears, as the coach of the Chicago Bears and as a player for the Chicago Bears. He played and/or coached the Bears to six NFL Championships. He was named coach of the year twice. He was selected to the 1920s All-Decade Team. His number 7 jersey is retired. He retired with a .671 winning percentage as a coach. He served in World War I and World War II, earning the Bronze Star.

Always give your best effort. What could you add to your résumé by doing so? Let's see—victory over cancer, hero, captain of the cancer survivors... Give it your best and see what happens!

DAY 293

Accept the challenges so that you can feel the exhilaration of victory.
—George S. Patton, 1885-1945
United States Army General

General Patton never stepped down from a challenge: the invasion of Casablanca, invasion of Sicily, armored attacks on Nazi Germany in France, his famous relief of American troops at Bastogne during the Battle of the Bulge, and his armored advance into Germany. Patton became an American folk hero by his actions in World War II.

You don't have to be as flamboyant as General Patton, but you can still feel the exhilaration of victory if you complete this journey with cancer. You took up this challenge days ago, now you need to keep pushing until its completion. Then you can claim victory and have the greatest feeling of your life.

DAY 294

If you haven't got any charity in your heart, you have the worst kind of heart trouble.
—Bob Hope, 1903-2003
American Comedian & Actor

Well said, Mr. Hope. He gave so many people *hope* with his charity work, especially the USO. He brought hope to our troops for six decades. Some of those USO tours took him very, very close to the front lines of war zones. He wasn't born American but became one of the most famous Americans because of his charity work. Giving money isn't the only way to show charity. Giving of time and love is of great value as well.

Your team members showed their charity when they joined you on your journey. They have no heart troubles at all! Hopefully there are others you know that were not able to help directly with you, but because of you, they made donations to a cancer charity or foundation, like the Avery Foundation.

DAY 295

Miracles happen every day; change your perception of what a miracle is and you'll see them all around you.
—Jon Bon Jovi, 1962-present
American Singer-Songwriter

As a cancer patient, you dream and hope for miracles every day, as do your families and loved ones. Maybe if you do as Bon Jovi said, you will see little miracles every day that will give you the strength to get a huge miracle down the road of your journey. Open your mind, heart, and eyes and you may find these miracles and help you with your journey!

DAY 296

Failure at some point in life is inevitable, but giving up is unforgivable.
—Joe Biden, 1942-present
47th Vice President of the United States

As a cancer patient, you will have some setbacks, small failures. Just don't give up. Learn from those setbacks and move on. There is too much at stake to just throw up your hands and say, "I give." Do you know how French children play army? They throw up their hands and say, "We surrender!" If you're French, I apologize. It is just a good joke. Don't be like the French children. Move on to fight another day.

Mr. Biden knows all about the setbacks and small failures during the journey with cancer. As Vice President of the United States, he lost his son Beau on May 30, 2015 from brain cancer. Beau never gave up and fought 'til the end.

DAY 297

Build up your weaknesses until they become your strong points.
　　　　　　　　—Knute Rockne 1888-1931
　　Norwegian-American College Football Coach

Rockne practiced these words as coach of the University of Notre Dame Fighting Irish. Many consider Rockne one of the greatest coaches in college football history. The College Football Hall of Fame says, "Without question, American Football's most renowned coach." His Irish teams won three National Championships and had five undefeated seasons. Rockne has the highest winning percentage of all college coaches at .881. His record was 105 wins, 12 losses and five ties. Rockne turned his team's weaknesses into strong points to earn all the before mentioned.

Ronald J. Avery

As you journey, take your weaknesses and make them strong points. Like turning any fear into courage. Flipping a negative thought into a positive. Turning weakness into determination. Taking bleakness and making hope for better tomorrows. Erasing "I don't care" with faith. Washing away dislike with love. Go win your championship!

DAY 298

Spring is God's way of saying, "One more time!"
—Robert Orben, 1927-present
American Comedy Writer

May there be plenty of springs on your journey with cancer. That every day is spring when you open your eyes. You are renewed each day like the flowers of spring and the green grass. You feel like you have new life, like the baby robins in their nest. You are filled with hope like the rainbow after the spring showers. Keep telling yourself, "One more time!"

DAY 299

We exaggerate misfortune and happiness alike. We are never either so wretched or so happy as we say we are.
—Honore De Balzac, 1799-1850
French Novelist

I completely disagree with Mr. De Balzac! I don't think a cancer patient exaggerates his or her misfortune. I don't think it is possible to exaggerate that. Don't ever let someone think that or assume that. They have not walked in your shoes and know not what they are talking about. I also disagree with the happiness. For a cancer patient that beats the beast, enjoys the greatest of life, which is life itself. That is not exaggerated, either. I think I will cross off my reading list any books by De Balzac.

DAY 300

> *Faced with crisis, the man of character falls back on himself. He imposes his own stamp on action, takes responsibility for it, makes it his own... difficulty attracts the man of character because it is in embracing it that he realizes himself.*
> —Charles De Gaulle, 1890-1970
> French General & Statesman

You were faced with a crisis when you received your diagnosis. You have imposed your own stamp on action, have taken responsibility for it, and made it your own. You have character; there is no doubt about that. Because you have embraced this crisis and you are taking it on. You will find yourself on this journey like never before. You will learn great things about yourself. You will have a better understanding of your faith, hope, and love. You will find strength you did not know you had. You will be a better person at journey's end.

DAY 301

We are not interested in the possibilities of defeat. They do not exist.
—Queen Victoria, 1819-1901
Queen of England

As a cancer patient, you should never be interested in the possibility of defeat. It should not exist for you. Think of that daily when you're getting out of bed. That should start your day out positively and lead you on a path to your daily victory. Take the word *defeat* out of your vocabulary and never use it in Scrabble. Make the word extinct.

DAY 302

Keep your face towards the sunshine and you cannot see a shadow.
—Helen Keller, 1880-1968
American Author

Keep looking up and forward never behind. That shadow is cancer and you don't want him to catch you. Noting behind you can change, so there is no need to look back there. Keep yourself focused on your journey and what needs to be done. Your journey does not go back in time. They have yet to make a time machine to do so—insert laugh and smile. Take care of today and make plans for tomorrow. Keep that shadow ever at your back!

DAY 303

Find a place inside where there's joy and the joy will burn out the pain.
—Joseph Campbell, 1904-1987
American Writer

Find some joy within you every day. As Mr. Campbell would say, "Follow your bliss." That is his simple philosophy for life. I, myself, like it a lot. Life as we know is way too short, so follow your bliss only makes sense, right? It's not hard to find bliss and joy. It's out there every day. It could be a number of different things for you: watching your favorite sports team, playing with your dog, visiting the grandchildren, going to a movie, looking at family pictures from the past, and many, many more ways. One way that always brings me joy is giving a young child a quarter. Watch their face light up like the Christmas tree at Rockefeller Center. It will burn out the pain out of anything! Find your joy and burn your pain away!

DAY 304

No matter what you're going through, there's a light at the end of the tunnel and it may seem hard to get to it, but you can do it and just keep working towards it and you'll find the positive side of things.
—Demi Lovato, 1992-present
American Singer-Songwriter

Demi has hit the nail right on the head here. Darn near what I would say exactly to the word. There is a light at the end of your tunnel. I know some days it may not seem like it, but it is there. Don't let the evil beast block it from you. Keep pushing ever forward day by day with positive thoughts and positive actions. Your light will get bigger and brighter. The next thing you know, you are right there at the light!

DAY 305

Few things in the world are more powerful than a positive push. A smile. A word of optimism and hope. A "you can do it" when things are tough.
—Richard M. DeVos, 1926-present
American Businessman

BY this time of your journey you are ready for a positive push. This is the time you need your team to step up to the plate and deliver for you. Bring a smile to your face. Give you encouragement and hope. Telling you "you can do it!" Give you optimism for better days ahead. Hug you with the love you need. Giving you a positive pep talk that gives you faith that you will be successful. Share this quote with your team!

DAY 306

Start by doing what's necessary, then do what's possible and suddenly you are doing the impossible.
—Francis of Assisi, 1182-1226
Italian Catholic Friar

You started your journey by doing what was necessary according to your physician's plan. Those small steps of necessity led you to take a bit bigger steps of what was possible. Then suddenly you are closing in on the impossible, the end of your journey. Taking bigger steps as the finish line is in sight. It can be done; you know that. You have seen others do it. So why can't you? The only thing that will stop you is you. And your team won't let that happen! It's time to start taking bigger steps!

DAY 307

Once you replace negative thoughts with positive ones, you'll start having positive results.
—Willie Nelson, 1933-present
American Singer-Songwriter

Positivity, positivity, positivity! So very important. Not just for you in this journey, but for everyone every day. Don't let negative thoughts creep their way into your journey or mind. They do not have a ticket for this journey and they are not going to freeload on your back. Stay positive at all times. It creates a barricade around you to keep all negativity away. Don't let your guard down. If you feel you are slipping, call on a team member to get you set back in place. Positivity, positivity, positivity!

DAY 308

The worst thing that happens to you may be the best thing for you if you don't let it get the best of you.
—Will Rogers, 1879-1935
American Actor

Cancer, I'm safe to assume, is the worst thing that has happened to you. It very well could be the best thing that has happened to you if you don't let it get the best of you. Getting through this difficult journey will lead to a better you at the end. A better you for better todays and tomorrows. If you can battle cancer and come out cancer-free, you will see your confidence soar like an eagle in the sky. Your self-worth will not be calculable it will be so high. You will have the courage to wrestle bears. Not real bears, a Chicago Bear; they are pretty easy to beat. Insert your daily laugh and smile! Your attitude will be so positive, you won't remember what negative is. Your faith will be so strong that your pastor may ask you to preach on Sunday.

DAY 309

When you go through a significant injury and have a major career change, you truly do go

one year at a time and you don't look past what's going on now, because you are not sure what's going to happen. Tomorrow is not promised.
—Payton Manning, 1976-present
American Professional Football Player

You are going through cancer right now and have had a major life change. You truly do go one day at a time, and you don't look past what's going on now, because you are not sure what's going to happen. Tomorrow is not promised. For you, that "tomorrow is not promised" hits home a little more than in the context Payton used it. Again, we hear about staying focused on what is happening right now. Don't be distracted and don't look too far ahead. If you do, what is happening right now could change negatively for you. Remember, one day at a time, step by step with little daily victories. The next thing you know, your journey will be complete.

DAY 310

Believe you can and you're half way there.
—Theodore Roosevelt, 1858-1919
26th President of the United States

Roosevelt believed he and his Rough Riders could bring victory home in the Spanish-American War. That belief leads the Americans to victory and made Theodore Roosevelt a war hero, which helped help him gain the governorship of New York, then the vice presidency and then the presidency of the United States. Roosevelt always believed in himself. He is regarded as one of the five best presidents.

What can that belief do for you? Keep believing and you're half way there. Get halfway there and continue to believe and guess what? You're on the home front of your journey. Don't ever give up on the belief that you can complete this journey. You can do it and you will do it, I'm sure.

DAY 311

> *If you believe in yourself and have dedication and pride—and never quit, you'll be a winner. The price of victory is high, but so are the rewards.*
> —Paul Bryant, 1913-1983
> American College Football Coach

Believe in yourself because we believe in you. Our belief in you will give you the pride you need. Your team will make sure you stay dedicated to the task at hand and never quit. This is not an easy battle and it is not a short battle. You must be dedicated to the long haul. Many have gone before you into this battle. Some have come out as complete victors and others have not. But they all came out as winners. As a victor your reward is the highest reward of all: life. Making the journey and not being a complete victor still makes you a hero and leaves us your legacy!

DAY 312

When you get into a place and everything goes against you, 'til it seems as though you could not hang on a minute longer, never give up then, for that is just the place and time that the tide will turn.
—Harriet Beecher Stowe, 1811-1896
American Author

You have heard it many different ways in this book: never give up! Never give up! Never give up! You can do this. Your team has you on their shoulders. The momentum is building for you even if you think you are at the end. The tide will turn and better days are ahead. So, keep giving it your best and push forward.

A good example of this is the beleaguered American troops in the Battle of the Bulge that were encircled by the Nazi German troops. They thought all hope was lost and they couldn't hold out any longer. Then out of nowhere through the forest comes General Patton and his Third Army Armored Division to save the troops and turn the tide of that battle.

It happens every day somewhere to someone. Hang on; your day will come.

DAY 313

A champion is someone who gets up when he can't.
　　　　　　　—Jack Dempsy, 1895-1983
　　　　　　　American Professional Boxer

You are a *champion!* Every day you get up to battle cancer. Some of those days you can't get up, but you do. Knowing what your task at hand is and that you cannot waste a minute. Some days the strength is weak and the pain is great. You still rise to the occasion, making you champion of all champions. There is no greater battle in life than the battle you are in right now, the battle for life!

In September of 1926 Jack was defending his Heavy Weight Championship against Gene Tunney. Jack lost the match and his title in that fight. When he spoke to his wife after the fight, Jack said these now famous words: "Honey, I forgot to duck." Those same words used fifty-five years later when President Ronald Reagan was shot and he spoke to his wife. Jack stood to fight another day, being the champion he was.

Remember, you are a champion. Don't give cancer your title belt!

DAY 314

The best way out is always through.
—Robert Frost, 1874-1963
American Poet

Stay on the straight and narrow path, right through the evil beast, cancer. Follow that same path through, as many cancer patients have before you. They have left their marks along the way for you to follow. Don't try to go around. Don't try to go under. Don't try to go over. You need to go straight through. There is no detour on this journey. To get to the end, you must go through the evil beast. If you try to go around, under, or over, you will get lost and cancer will eat you up. *Straight* through!

DAY 315

I have always believed, and I still believe, that whatever good or bad fortune may come our way, we can always give it meaning and transform it into something of value.
—Hermann Hesse 1877—1962
German Poet

Bad fortune has come your way, but if you stay positive, show courage, hope, and determination, you will overcome this and transform it into something positive and of great value.

It is like what the people of this country did for Houston in the summer of 2017 after their devastating floods. People from all over the country went to help the citizens of Houston. People that couldn't go gave donations of food, water, clothing, and money. People in the surrounding towns came with their fishing boats to help make water rescues. The people of Houston didn't give up. They all showed great courage to get through those floods without a large loss of lives. Everyone came together to take this bad fortune of Houston and transform it into something of value and special. So many stories of good will. The people rallied!

Your team has rallied around you to help you through your bad fortune. Embrace them and work hard to get through this. We know you can.

DAY 316

Nurture your minds with great thoughts. To believe in the heroic makes heroes.
—Benjamin Disraeli, 1804-1881
British Prime Minister

Become our hero. Nurture your mind with great thoughts during your journey. To believe you can slay the evil beast, cancer. You can, we know you can, because you are our hero! Like Enrique Iglesias song *Hero* says, "Let me be your hero. Would you dance if I asked you to dance? Would you run and never look back? Would you cry if you saw me crying? Would you save my soul tonight?" Be our hero!

DAY 317

Look within. Within is the fountain of good and it will ever bubble up, if thou wilt ever dig.
—Marcus Aurelius, 121 AD-180 AD
Roman Emperor

Look deep within yourself. Dig deeper and you will find your fountain of good. This fountain of good will sustain you during your journey. Just keep letting it bubble up. Allowing it to bubble up will keep washing away any and all negative thoughts that try to creep in.

DAY 318

The most authentic thing about us is our capacity to create, to overcome, to endure, to transform, to love, and to be greater than our suffering.
—Ben Okari, 1959-present
Nigerian Poet

You have the capacity to overcome and endure. You will transform yourself during this journey to come out in the end a better person. The capacity of your family and friends, their love with you, will give you the strength needed for the whole journey. You will endure this and overcome the suffering. Jim and Julie both created, overcame, endured, transformed, and loved—making their suffering much less. They passed of course, but they were much greater than their suffering at the end!

DAY 319

Failure will never overtake me if my determination to succeed is strong enough.
—Og Mandino, 1923-1996
American Author

Be very, very determined. You can do this! Do not let anything or anyone try to erode your determination. Look at the determination Martin Luther King, Jr. had throughout his lifetime to bring civil rights to all people of this country. Failure never overtook him or his movement. His nonviolent tactics, inspired by Gandhi, were heroic in the face of violence from the opposition. That tactic won him the 1964 Nobel Peace Prize. His determination never wavered through all the violence thrown at them. His determination was very evident in Washington D.C. in 1963 when he gave his famous "I Have a Dream" speech to thousands and thousands of people. His determination carried on even after his assassination in 1968.

Stay determined through your pain and suffering. Like Mr. King did through all the violence thrown at him. Don't give failure a chance.

DAY 320

If you can dream it, you can do it.
—Walt Disney, 1901-1966
American Entrepreneur

Dream every night about life after cancer. What happiness you will have. Where you are going to go? Who are you going to see? What are you going to do? Remember the old Disney commercials right after the Super Bowl and World Series? A voice would say, "Payton Manning, you just won the Super Bowl. Where are you going to go?" Payton would look at the camera and say, "I'm going to Disney World!" Make that your dream! It is the happiest place in the world!

Just look at Mr. Disney's dream and what it has turned into! He had a dream and made it reality! And that dream still grows bigger and bigger every year. He has made billions upon billions of children so very happy with his dream. I know I have taken my children there several times! Yes, it is the greatest place in world for children.

Dream it!

DAY 321

Nothing is impossible, the word itself says "I'm possible"!
—Audrey Hepburn, 1929-1993
British-Belgian Actress

Hepburn knows this because she lived it early in her life. Her family was living in the Netherlands when Nazi Germany took over the country. She saw many Jewish children her age being hauled away on trains to concentration camps. She witnessed executions by Nazi troops right in the streets. In 1944 the Nazis blocked the supply routes of food and fuel into the Netherlands. Her family had to make flour from tulip bulbs for cake and biscuits. Hepburn developed acute anemia, respiratory problems, and edema from malnutrition. Her family did not use the word *impossible*. They made things possible to get through this most difficult time. From there she went on to make herself one of the most famous actresses of her time. In her later life she devoted a lot of time to UNICEF and received the Presidential Medal of Freedom for that work. She truly believed "I'm possible"!

You, too are possible. Say it to yourself, "I'm possible!" Say it again on your hard days. You will always be possible! Your completion of your journey is possible. Nothing should impossible, right?

DAY 322

Memories of our lives, of our works and our deeds will continue in others.
—Rosa Parks, 1913-2005
First Lady of Civil Rights

Our foundation, the Avery Foundation, is for the memories and legacies of James D. Avery and Julie M. Avery. Their works and deeds will continue with us at this Foundation. Their memory will never die.

What will be the memory of your life? Will others carry your banner when you pass? We all hope that your passing won't be anytime soon and won't be from this terrible cancer within you. You do need to think about this, tough. None of us are guaranteed a certain number of days here. Make sure your works and deeds will continue with others. Leave a legacy for future generations. Let your torch be carried forever.

DAY 323

All you need is the plan, the road map, and the courage to press on to your destination.
—Earl Nightingale, 1921-1989
American Author

You have the plan your physicians laid out for you at the start of this journey. Make sure you didn't lose it. Make sure you review it. Make sure you understand it. With that plan came your road map. Again, make sure you didn't lose it. Make sure you review it. Because this destination will *not* show up on your GPS system. Keep showing your great courage to press on, because you have not reached the end of this journey yet. Don't stop, don't hesitate; just forward you go.

DAY 324

No act of kindness, no matter how small, is ever wasted.
—Aesop, 600 BC-564 BC
Greek Fabulist

Be open to all acts of kindness towards you. Many small acts add up to a big act. Kindness shown to you is valuable to your journey. It gives you a jolt of energy and brings happiness to your heart and soul. It could be as simple as a smile from the mailman, someone opening a door for you, your kid or friend getting you something to drink so you don't have to get up, a phone call from a loved one, someone telling you to have a great day, etc. Take them and put them in your bank. You can never have enough of them.

DAY 325

People say it's not ambitious, but it is actually quite ambitious wanting to help people.
—Prince William, 1982-present
Duke of Cambridge

Anyone that takes of their own time to help others is very, very ambitious. Thank your team members since they are doing exactly this for you. Someday you will have the opportunity to return the favor to someone. Prince William learned this from his mother, Princess Diana. She was very involved in helping others. She instilled this into her two sons, Prince William and Prince Harry. Nobody is above helping others. In fact, those with the most should help the most.

DAY 326

If you want a happy ending, that depends, of course, on where you stop your journey.
—Orson Wells, 1915-1985
American Actor & Director

Orson, being the director he was, could stop the journey where he wanted to produce the ending he needed in his films. You are the actor, the producer, the director, and writer of your film. Where are you going to stop your journey? Will it be a happy ending that we all want? Is the film going to be a cliffhanger? I hope it isn't a horror film! I would go with an epic film. Hopefully you control this whole movie and a new director and producer (cancer) doesn't take over, so you can determine the ending. And you better make it happy!

DAY 327

If you live long enough, you'll make mistakes. But if you learn from them, you'll be a better person. It's how you handle adversity, not how it affects you. The main thing is never quit, never quit, never quit.
—Bill Clinton, 1946-present
42nd President of the United States

Those words again, never quit! It can't be said enough. Yes, you will have setbacks, failures, mistakes as your journey goes along. Handle these adversities with grace and confidence that you will overcome them. Learning from them and then overcoming them makes you a better person. Use them as the learning tool that they can be. Do not let them affect you negatively.

President Clinton handled adversity as president of the United States, which all presidents have to, but he seemed to have a little more than most. Some of that was of his own doing. He never let it get in the way governed. He was president during the nation's longest period of economic expansion in American history. He was the first democrat to be elected to a second term since Franklin Roosevelt. He was responsible for welfare reform. His last three years in office, his budget had a surplus, for the first time since 1969. He left office with the highest approval rating of any president since World War II. President Clinton not only handled adversity, he threw it right away. He by no means ever quit!

Keep a firm handle on your adversity. Never quit, never quit, never quit.

DAY 328

With self-discipline most anything is possible.
—Theodore Roosevelt, 1858-1919
26th President of the United States

You need to be self-disciplined to stay the course on your journey with cancer. Don't try to take any shortcuts or think another way is better than what your physicians gave you. Stay the course, straight ahead. As you know, the path can get curvy and dark, muddy and full of potholes. You still must stay the course. Be self-disciplined to stay positive during those times and keep the faith. Make this journey possible!

President Roosevelt stayed self-disciplined with his policies. Pushing policies through as a progressive that were labeled "The Square Deal". These policies were not popular by the large companies of his day. Many of the rich owners were not happy with the president. These policies helped the average citizens of our country. He remained self-disciplined in the face of threats from big business. He made it possible!

You can make this journey possible! We know you can.

DAY 329

We shall drain from the heart of suffering itself the means of inspiration and survival.
—Winston Churchill, 1874-1965
British Prime Minister

Sir Winston has so many inspirational words for us. If we could bring him back and have him personally talk to each cancer patient, they would be filled with all the courage, inspiration, and bravery needed to kick cancer out of their lives. He could make an atheist a believer. He could make a Democrat a Republican. I wonder if he could make water wine? No, no that was Jesus. Churchill almost single-handedly kept up the spirits of the British people during their darkest hours of World War II. Where would this world be today if Churchill didn't rally the Brits and keep Nazi Germany from further expansion? Would we be speaking German right now?

Keep draining from the heart of your suffering your means of inspiration and survival. It will get better at some point. Hang in there like the Brits did during the many, many days of the London bombings. Google Winston Churchill's "We shall never surrender" speech and listen to it. If that does not rally you, nothing will.

By the way, this is one of my all-time favorite quotations. I used it a lot in TV, radio, and newspaper interviews about our Foundation. It is sort of our rallying call as well.

DAY 330

If I can stop one heart from breaking, I shall not live in vain; if I can ease one life the aching, or cool one pain, or help one fainting robin unto his nest again, I shall not live in vain.
— Emily Dickinson, 1830-1886
American Poet

Avery Foundation version:

If I can stop one cancer patient's heart from breaking, I shall not live in vain; if I can ease one cancer patient's aching, or cool one pain, or help them back into their chair again, I shall not live in vain.

We hope your team feels this exact way as well, which I'm sure they do. They are right by your side and only want the best for you. Let them know their actions do not go unnoticed. They do not want to live in vain.

DAY 331

Cancer can take away all my physical abilities. It cannot touch my mind, it cannot touch my heart, and it cannot touch my soul.
—Jimmy Valvano, 1946-1993
American College Basketball Coach

Well said, coach! Don't let the evil beast get into your mind. Don't let it break your heart. Don't let it blacken your soul. Keep telling yourself exactly what Jimmy V said. He lost his life to cancer, but not his heart, soul or mind. He did not lose either. He was victorious over cancer. He has been inspirational to thousands of cancer patients. It cannot be counted, but I'm sure his inspiration has saved lives of cancer patients. Cancer thought it won when he passed, but no way. Jimmy V is getting the last laughs as he puts smiles back onto so many sad faces. Like a Jedi, he is more powerful dead than alive. I think he may be a distant cousin of Yoda. Insert smile and laugh for the day.

DAY 332

We have but one life here... It pays, no matter what comes after it, to try and do things, to accomplish things in this life, and not merely to have a soft and pleasant time.
—Theodore Roosevelt, 1858-1919
26th President of the United States

You need to have purpose in your life! You need to leave a legacy behind so you will always be with us in memory. Having a soft and pleasant time is not a legacy. You will be erased from everyone's mind a week after they bury you. Jim and Julie both believed in this and have left their legacies and memories with us forever. They accomplished so much during their journey with cancer. When they found out that it was terminal, they did even more so they could accomplish things they felt important before they passed. Just keep grinding, keep accomplishing, keep making memories for us!

DAY 333

I know God will not give me anything I can't handle... I just wish he didn't test me so much.
—Saint Teresa of Calcutta, 1910-1997
Albanian-Indian Catholic Saint

I'm sure you feel what Saint Teresa is saying. But, be glad in that God won't give you more than you can handle. Stay calm throughout with this knowledge. Continue to follow the path that is laid out for you. Always forward. God has tested you greatly with this one. Now trust in him that you will handle it!

Saint Teresa handled a lot for God. In 1950, with a blessing from the Vatican, she started the Missionaries of Charity. By the time of her death in 1997, the Missionaries of Charity had 610 missions in 123 countries! How could she handle that? Well, she did because God knew she could do it. She brought God's work to 123 countries. Helping the poor and the sick. Saint Teresa saved so many, many lives with her missions throughout the world. She was tested each time the Missionaries of Charity grew to more missions and more countries. Her charity work never skipped a beat as it grew. She handled it and she trusted in God that she could.

You can handle it; trust in God!

DAY 334

Hope is the power of being cheerful in circumstances that we know to be desperate.
—G.K. Chesterton, 1874-1936
English Poet & Philosopher

You have had hope all the way through this journey of yours. Hope is what a cancer patient must grasp firmly and never let go of, because we know the cancer makes things a bit desperate. Your hope feeds your positive attitude, your determination, your faith, and even your strength. You lose hope and the dominos will start to fall. Stay cheerful as you can during this journey and the flames of hope will continue to burn!

DAY 335

Take one day at a time. Today, after all, is the tomorrow you worried about yesterday.
—Billy Graham, 1918-present
American Christian Evangelist

One day, one victory at a time day by day. Just keep rolling them out. Don't look back at yesterday; it's over and you cannot change it. Don't worry about tomorrow, because you need to worry about today and what is at hand right now. Don't let your mind get over crowded with history and the future. Keep it clear for the now! You keep moving forward, but don't look out forward. Important for you to concentrate all energies on today. Making sure that today will be a small victory, one of many on your journey. One day at a time, just like the television show of the 1970s.

DAY 336

It does not matter how long you live, but how well you live.
　　　—Martin Luther King Jr., 1929-1968
　　　American Baptist Minister & Activist

Seems very sad that Mr. King said these words and then was assassinated at the young age of 39. But, he did live well. He was an inspiration to millions across the world. His work for civil rights is legendary. He won the Nobel Peace Prize in 1964 for his civil rights work. He was awarded the Presidential Medal of Freedom in 1977, posthumous. He also awarded the Congressional Gold Medal in 2004, posthumous. We have a national holiday in his honor around his birthday in January. He led many nonviolent marches and campaigns during the 1960s for civil rights. He packed a lot into just

39 years and touched many people in the best possible way. I remember as a kid reading his "I Have a Dream" speech over and over again. It was so powerful and I swear I felt something inside me when I read it; something good.

Don't spend time worrying about how long you will live. You don't have any time for that. You need to worry about your journey and how to live the best you can along the way. Make sure you leave good memories and as I have said before, leave a legacy!

DAY 337

The best revenge is massive success.
—Frank Sinatra, 1915-1998
American Singer & Actor

Take some revenge out on the cancer that interrupted your life. Show no mercy on it. Massive success would be daily victories for you. Make progress every day without losing ground to this evil beast. Take it day by day with success after success. You continue that and you will have that massive success. Stick with it and don't lose your hope! Nothing tastes better than a revenge burger and fries!

DAY 338

I intend to live forever or die trying.
　　　—Groucho Marx, 1890-1977
　　　　American Comedian

The typical quick wit from one of the greatest comedians of all time. He almost lived forever; 86 years. He may have lived longer if he didn't love those cigars so much. What is forever, anyhow? Do we really know? Groucho just wanted to live as long as he could. Like all of us do. There is nothing wrong with being a lover of life! Groucho once said, "Anyone can get old—all you have to do is live long enough."

Well here's looking at you over my Groucho glasses and nose, hoping you live long enough to get old. You can use this line on yourself to get yourself motivated for the day. Life for you is a little more fragile and forever seems like it could be around the corner. Well, it won't be if you keep up your hard work and effort to beat this!

DAY 339

It's not complicated to embrace life. You just have to make a choice.
　　　—Faith Hill, 1967-present
　　　　American Singer-Songwriter

Cancer can make embracing life complicated if you let it, but don't! Make the choice to embrace it. Every moment of it. This will mentally help you so much on your journey. Puts you in the frame of mind you need to stay positive and make progress. Some days it is mind over matter, as you well know. You have the choice to embrace life and to fight for your life. A lot of people don't get that choice. Think of all the people in the World Trade Centers when they went down. Think of all the people at the concert in Las Vegas. Think about all the people at the Pulse nightclub in Orlando. Think about all the people at Virginia Tech. Think about all the children at Sandy Hook Elementary School. Think about all the children at Columbine High School. This list could go on for a long time. I think you get what I'm saying. Embrace life and fight for it!

DAY 340

Above anything else, I hate to lose.
    —Jackie Robinson, 1919-1972
  American Professional Baseball Player

Nobody likes to lose. I don't care what you say, nobody does. What do you think Mr. Robinson thinks about giving out participation trophies? We all need to learn how to win and how to lose. But the facts are that losing sucks. You need to put forth the effort to win. I hope you hate to lose! I do *not* like to use the word "hate". When talking about cancer, I have no problem using the word. Use your dislike of losing to motivate you to following your plan and never giving up. Just like Mr. Robinson, you have a strong team around to help you make sure you don't lose.

DAY 341

The greatest evil is physical pain.
—Saint Augustine, 354 AD-430 AD
Roman African Catholic Saint

And now you know why I have referred to cancer as the "evil beast" throughout this book. To see the pain it brought to my brother and sister brought me pain. It is truly the evil beast. It makes me furious just thinking about it. I can clearly see in my mind Jim and Julie laying in their beds overwhelmed by pain and unable to talk. Damn you, cancer!

Do your best every day to avoid the physical pain this beast can bring you. Better yet, slay the evil beast!

DAY 342

Good is not good when better is expected.
—Vince Scully, 1927-present
American Sportscaster

Good is not good enough when battling cancer. Better is what you should hold yourself to, so you can complete this journey. Do the best job you can, good should not be on your radar. Better and best is what you need to focus on. Vince, being the longtime voice of the Los Angeles Dodgers, can tell you that good teams don't make the World Series. Better teams are the ones that win championships.

Your team is better! Go get yourself a championship!

DAY 343

To make no mistakes is not in the power of man, but from their errors and mistakes the wise and good learn wisdom for the future.
—Plutarch, 46 AD-120 AD
Greek Biographer

You may have or will have some mistakes or errors on your journey. You learn from them and keep moving forward. You don't make those mistakes or errors again, because, like Plutarch said, you're wise and good! I always tried to teach my kids to take ownership of their mistakes and use them as a learning tool. I did the same with young managers that worked for me. When you don't take ownership, you won't learn from them. Your journey will be much easier if you are wise and good!

DAY 344

You should never view your challenges as a disadvantage. Instead, it's important for you to understand that your experience facing and overcoming adversity is actually one of your biggest advantages.
—Michelle Obama, 1964-present
Former First Lady of the United States

I throw these exact words out to my friend Russ, who will have to start treatments for his cancer again. He has the experience of beating this once before and he will do it again! Fight on, Russ! He has overcome this adversity once and will use it to his advantage to beat it again.

Fight on, any of you who have to fight the fight again! Remember that your experience will be to your advantage! Don't back down and take it to the evil beast!

DAY 345

Only if you have been in the deepest valley can you ever know how magnificent it is to be on the highest mountain.
—Richard Nixon, 1913-1994
37th President of the United States

You will travel through the deepest valley on your journey. That tall mountain off in the distance is your light at the end of the tunnel. Your life may be magnificent when you reach its top. For that is the end of your long, tough journey. Don't give up, keep pushing onward and upward to the mountain top!

President Nixon knew all too well the deepest valley and the highest mountain in his political career. That career took off rapidly in 1946 when he was elected a congressman for California. Then in 1950 he was elected a senator for California. Then in 1952 Dwight Eisenhower picked Nixon as his running mate for the presidential campaign. Nixon was Vice President of the United States for eight years. Almost at the top of the mountain. He won the Republican presidential nomination in 1960 and ran against John F. Kennedy. He lost a close election and tumbled down the mountain side. Then in 1962 he lost a bid to become governor of California. Putting him in deepest valley far from the mountain top. Then in 1968 he again won the Republican nomination for president and defeated Hubert Humphrey. He made it to that mountain top and remained there into his second term as president. Then he tumbled again with the Watergate scandal, which lead to him resigning as president. The only president to ever do so. He was in the valley, up near the top of the mountain, then back down, then to the mountain top and finally back down. Makes me dizzy just trying to explain this.

When you reach that mountain top, plan on staying up there. Don't do the Nixon bounce!

DAY 346

I think you need to go through some stuff to really appreciate life and understand what it means to persevere, overcome, and have faith. I think those tough times make you a stronger person.

—Judith Hill, 1984-present
American Singer-Songwriter

The tough times you are going through now will surely make you appreciate life. You will persevere and overcome with your strong faith in yourself and your team. At the end of this journey you will be a stronger person. Tough times bring out the best in a lot of people. Stick to it and you could see the best in you come forth.

DAY 347

Success is to be measured not so much by the position that one has reached in life as by the obstacles which he has overcame.
—Booker T. Washington, 1856-1915
American Author

Well then, Booker T. Washington was a very, very successful man. He was born into slavery and rose from that to become one of the most influential African-Americans. He was the leader of the African-American community. He was an educator at the Tuskegee Institute in Alabama. He was an author. He was an advisor to the presidents of the United States. He was the founder of the National Negro Business League. Just think of the obstacles he overcame in his era to reach these accomplishments.

Your success will be measured by how you handle this obstacle of cancer. You have made it this far on your journey and you can make it from here to the end. Regardless of the outcome, your journey will be successful. Just as Jim's and Julie's was. Keep pushing and keep your faith!

DAY 348

I know not age, nor weariness nor defeat.
—Rose Kennedy, 1890-1995
American Philanthropist

Mrs. Kennedy lived these very words. She had a long life, 104 years, filled with many ups and downs. She never let age be a factor as to what she did. She was very involved in many charitable groups. She outlived four of her children. She was mother to a president, John F., and two senators, Robert and Ted. Both John and Robert were killed by assassins. No weariness stopped her through those troubled times. She was the matriarch of the Kennedy Family.

This is another good quotation to write down and read each morning. Let it give you hope for better days!

DAY 349

Prayer is not asking. Prayer is putting oneself in the hands of God, at his disposition, and listening to his voice in the depth of our hearts.
—Saint Teresa of Calcutta, 1910-1997
Albanian-Indian Catholic Saint

Prayer is good. Prayer is good for your mind. Prayer can make a difference for you, if you allow it to. *Focus on the Family* tells us twelve reasons to pray:

1. God's word calls us to pray.
2. Jesus prayed regularly.
3. Prayer is how we communicate with God.
4. Prayer allows us to participate in God's works.
5. Prayer gives us power over evil.
6. Prayer is always available.
7. Prayer keeps us humble before God.
8. Prayer grants us the privilege of experiencing God.
9. Answered prayer is a potential witness.
10. Prayer strengthens the bonds between believers.
11. Prayer can succeed where other means have failed.
12. Prayer fulfills emotional needs.

For you, number five should give you all the reasons in the world to pray. Prayer gives us power over evil. Allow your prayer to give you power over the evil of cancer, the evil beast. Make prayer part of your daily routine. Prayer fulfills your emotional needs, as stated above in number twelve. Your emotional needs are great during this journey. Helping those needs is of utmost importance. My prayer for you is that I hope you believe in prayer and what it can do for you.

DAY 350

If you do not hope, you will not find what is beyond hopes.
—Saint Clement of Alexandra, 150 AD-215 AD
                                        Greek Theologian

Hope is what fuels your fire to battle your cancer daily. Hope is what eases your mind about your task at hand. Hope is what brings you dreams for better tomorrows. You must have hope in order to succeed on this journey. What is beyond hope for you? A better you that is cancer-free. That is what is beyond your hope. If you don't hope, beyond hope will never happen. Keep your faith strong in hope of better tomorrows, so at some point you can find it!

DAY 351

Time spent in nature decreases stress and anxiety and improve focus for adults as well as children.
—Laura Bush, 1946-present
Former First Lady of the United States

I can very well see where this is true. I know when I take a hike to the creek by our house through the woods, I feel like nothing can bother me. That I just walked into a protected dome of solitude and tranquility. All my stress left at the edge of the woods. I can just sit and listen to babbling creek and the birds. It's a very peaceful place, nature is. I leave there, stress free and ready to handle the next venture.

Make a trip to nature in your area. Take a hike and feel the stress from your journey fall from your shoulders. All the anxiety you have seems drained from your system. A feeling of peace will come over you. Well, as long as you don't get chased by a bear or something! Insert laugh and smile for your daily dose. Just take time to stop and listen to the music of nature. Can you hear the wind blowing through the leaves on the trees? How many different birds can you hear singing? Can you hear the babbling of the stream? Can you hear the frogs talking back and forth? Can you hear the crickets playing their orchestra for you? Let yourself get lost for a while. Then return more focused than ever for your journey!

DAY 352

You are not alone in this world. You are not alone with your problems.
—Unknown

Don't ever think you are alone in this and with your problems. That is why team is stressed so much here in this book. You have a team you assembled around for this journey. Keep them close. As part of that team, you have your physicians. Keep communication wide open with them. Ask questions and have understanding to put your mind at ease. Your problems have become all of their problems, as well. They will help you through this journey. If you're home alone and having a rough day, call a member of your team and invite them over for coffee. If you invite me, you will need to have Mountain Dew on hand! Don't ever feel like you're bothering someone when you call and ask for help or ask for some company. Share your problems with them and together a solution can be made!

DAY 353

Keep love in your heart. A life without is like a sunless garden when the flowers are dead.
—Oscar Wilde, 1854-1900
Irish Poet

You can never have enough love in your life. You can never give enough love in your lifetime. Love for you on this journey is the gasoline for your engine. Your team has given you love throughout your journey thus far, I hope. They will continue as your journey continues. You should be showing love to others as well. That love you give will multiple and come back onto you twofold. Love is something that feels wonderful, both giving and receiving. It should give you warmth inside. It will help keep your engine firing on all cylinders to reach journey's end. You don't want your garden of life to be sunless and filled with death. Love all and accept all love!

DAY 354

Successful people maintain a positive focus in life no matter what is going on around them. They stay focused on their past successes rather than their past failures and on the next action steps they need to get them closer to

the fulfillment of their goals, rather than all the other distractions that life presents to them.
—Jack Canfield, 1944-present
American Author

You want this journey to be a success, so keep your attitude positive until the end. Stay focused on your journey with distractions. Life does throw many distractions at you daily. It is hard to avoid them all. The biggest distraction is social media. It is addictive and very much a distraction to everyday life. It is easy to get lost in all the gossip, fake news, and whining that comes with it. You have no time for that and I hope you see that. Most social media sites have become just a place to gossip and vent negative filled rubbish. Your time would be better spent with family over a board game.

DAY 355

Life is a series of natural and spontaneous changes. Don't resist them—that only creates sorrow. Let reality be reality. Let things flow naturally forward in whatever way they like.
—Lao Tzu, 604 BC-531 BC
Chinese Philosopher

You know too well about life's natural and spontaneous changes. The change that has befallen you is one that is very hard to handle. It is reality though and you, nor anyone else can change that. As the saying goes, it is what it is. By feeling resentful or *why me*, you just create more sorrow for yourself, which is very unhealthy to be successful on your journey. Like you have read from me several times prior, always forward. Push through straight ahead. You can do this. You have gotten this far; nothing should stop you.

DAY 356

If you have no confidence in self, you are twice defeated in the race of life.
　　　　　　　　—Marcus Garvey, 1887-1940
　　　　　　　　Jamaican Political Leader

If you have no confidence in yourself that you can be successful on this journey, who will? How can anyone have confidence in you if you don't? All that team talk I have given throughout this book may as well have been written in invisible ink. Nobody wants to be on a team, with a lack for better words, of a known loser. It would be like offering a great NFL player to go play on the Cleveland Browns. The stakes cannot be any higher for you. Self-confidence is not an option on a menu board. It is a must have to complete this journey. If you lost yours, find it! If you got this far without, you best get to the store and buy some. If you think you need more, borrow some. Just have it!

DAY 357

The most difficult thing is the decision to act, the rest is merely tenacity. The fears are paper tigers. You can do anything you decide to do. You can act to change and control your life — and the procedure, the process is its own reward.
—Amelia Earhart, 1897-1937
American Aviation Pioneer

Amelia had tenacity; no doubt of that! She did anything she decided to do. And she was rewarded for those decisions. She showed no fear and had complete self-confidence. She never hesitated to act on her dreams. She was the first female to fly solo across the Atlantic Ocean. She held many aviation records. She formed an organization for female pilots, the Ninety-Nines. She stood up for women's political rights. She was a huge star of her time. The world lost her too early when trying to complete a flight around the world, she disappeared into the Pacific Ocean.

You made the difficult decision already by taking this journey with the hopes of a happy conclusion. Now, throughout the journey you must show tenacity and be committed to its completion. Fears are paper tigers that you need to convert to courage. You decided to do this, so you can do it! May there be the reward you want at the end!

DAY 358

If you love life, don't waste time, for time is what life is made of.
—Bruce Lee, 1940-1973
Chinese-American Actor

Little did Mr. Lee know how little time he had in his life: only 32 years. Time is so valuable! My dear sister Julie only had 21 years. Sometimes it just doesn't seem fair, but this is life and we do love it. Do not waste time. Your time must be used to fight the fight and find happiness as you do. Any distractions need to be checked at the door before they come into your house. Recruit one of your team members to be your doorman and ensure that. Time is life!

DAY 359

The greatest legacy one can pass on to one's children and grandchildren is not money or other material things accumulated in one's life, but rather the legacy of character and faith.
—Billy Graham, 1918-present
American Christian Evangelist

What do you want your legacy to be? Do you even want to leave a legacy? Maybe leaving the money and material goods will be good enough. *No, no, and no.* Of course, you want to leave a legacy. I almost think it is selfish not to leave a legacy for your children, grandchildren, and all family members. I think the only exceptions would be gangsters, professional thieves, drug addicts, and murderers. (You know the drill, insert laugh and smile here.)

Jim and Julie both left their legacies with us. They are of character, love, family, courage, bravery, faith, determination, and hope. I will carry their legacy with me forever and hope I can leave the same legacy for those after me. Your legacy is determined right now as you make this journey. Make it a hero's legacy that your children and grandchild can brag about for years to come.

DAY 360

To accomplish great things, we must not only act, but also dream; not only plan, but also believe.
—Antole France, 1844-1924
French Poet

I love, love this quotation. It tells you exactly what I have tried for 360 days and was unable to. I should have just started the book with this quotation, right? (Yes, insert laugh and smile). Dream of great things for yourself and act on that dream. Dream that you will walk out of your physician's office with a clean bill of health. Follow that plan and believe in that plan. Great things can happen! Ask any cancer survivor. It can be done as long as you dream it, plan it, act on it, and believe in it!

DAY 361

Bad things do happen; how I respond to them defines my character and the quality of my life. I can choose to sit in perpetual sadness, immobilized by the gravity of my loss, or I can choose to rise from the pain and treasure the most precious gift I have—life itself.
—Walter Anderson, 1903-1965
American Painter & Writer

Tell you something you don't know, right? Mr. Bad Thing knocked on your door some time ago. Your response to him was to fight the fight and take this journey. You are of great character and I'm sure your quality of life is much better than it would have been if you sat in perpetual sadness. Like Walter said, you would be immobilized by that. Thus, completely unable to take up this journey with any success. You have risen many days from pain to continue down this path. Nobody needs to tell you that. Sorry, I did; just trying to pat you on the back. Nice job by you and continue 'til the end. Your life is precious! And your life is a gift!

DAY 362

> *By prevailing over all obstacles and distractions, one may unfailingly arrive at his chosen goal or destination.*
> —Christopher Columbus, 1451-1506
> Italian Explorer

Upon completion of your journey, through and over all the obstacles, around all the distractions, you will arrive at your chosen goal and destination. That goal and destination of freedom from the evil beast, cancer! May this happen for you!

DAY 363

We've climbed the mighty mountain. I see the valley below and it's a valley of peace.
—George W. Bush, 1946-present
43rd President of the United States

May you reach the top of this mighty mountain. To let your eyes see the valley below of peace and tranquility. Where cancer has no place. It is there, waiting for you to arrive!

DAY 364

The boundaries which divide life from death are at best shadowy and vague. Who shall say where the ends, and where the other begins?

—Edgar Allen Poe, 1809-1849
American Poet

Those boundary lines between life and death for you are close together. Very shadowy, vague, and murky. If you stay positive, work hard, smile, have faith, and hope and determination, you will shed a light and make those lines very visible so you can see that line of death clearly and not cross it. Your journey does not need to end there. Push on!

DAY 365

The best way to predict the future is to create it.
—Peter Drucker, 1909-2005
Austrian-American Author

What will your future be with this cancer? Will you survive this battle? Will you come out victorious and healthy? You can create that future. Try to continue this journey with the suggestions I have left for you. We are all here for you and to help you reach your future that you want and dream of. Your courage, faith, and hope can carry you to that future. You can find strength in that! May God bless you!

2 Timothy 4:7

I have fought the good fight, I have finished the race, I have kept the faith.

Works Cited

Scott Hamilton. (Figure Skater). https://en.wikipedia.org/wiki/Scott_Hamilton_(figure_skater)

Barack Obama. https://en.wikipedia.org/wiki/Barack_Obama

Jack Nicklaus. https://www.pgatour.com/players/player.01869.Jack—Nicklaus.html

Tom Brady. https://en.wikipedia.org/wiki/Tom_Brady

Muhammad Ali. https://en.wikipedia.org/wiki/Muhammad_Ali

Romine, Brentley. "Arnold Palmer's golf career, by the numbers." Golfweek. 25 Sept. 2016. <golfweek.com/2016/09/25/Arnold—palmer—numbers—stats—pga—tour/>

Nelson Mandela. <https://en.wikipedia.org/wiki/Nelson_Mandela>

Vince Lombardi. https://www.pro—football—reference.com/coaches/LombVi0.htm

Colonel Sanders. https://en.wikipedia.org/wiki/Colonel_Sanders

Johnny Carson. https://en.wikipedia.org/wiki/Johnny_Carson

Daniel Boone. https://en.wikipedia.org/wiki/Daniel_Boone

Stephen Hawking. https://en.wikipedia.org/wiki/Stephen_Hawking

Wayne Gretzky. https://www.hockey—reference.com/players/g/gretzwa01.html

Dutta, Amit. "What are some examples of great mentors in the history of the world?" Quora. 28 Oct. 2014. https://www.quora.com/What—are—some—examples—of—great—mentors—in—the—history—of—the—world

Lou Brock. https://www.baseball—reference.com/players/b/brocklo01.shtml

Tim Tebow. https://en.wikipedia.org/wiki/Tim_Tebow

John Glenn. https://en.wikipedia.org/wiki/John_Glenn

Malala Yousafzai. https://en.wikipedia.org/wiki/Malala_Yousafzai

Ronald Reagan. https://www.archives.gov/publications/prologue/2007/summer/berlin.html

Serena Williams. https://en.wikipedia.org/Serena_Williams_career_statistics

The Blitz. https://en.wikipedia.org/wiki/The_Blitz

Foo Fighters. "Times Like These." https://www.azlyrics.com/lyrics/foofighters/timeslikethese.html

Wojiciechowski, Gene. "Game 6 delivers a true fall classic." ESPN. 28 Oct. 2011. https://www.espn.com/espn/columns/story?page=wojiciechowski—111027

1988 Notre Dame Fighting Irish Football Team. https://ipfs.io/ipfs/

365 Days for Hope

QmXoypizjW3WknFiJnKLwHCnL72vedxjQkDDP1m
XWo6uco/wiki/1988_Notre_Dame_Fighting_Irish_
football_team.html

Ulysses S. Grant. https://en.wikipedia.org/wiki/
Ulysses_S._Grant

John Wayne. https://en.wikipedia.org/wiki/John_Wayne

Robin Williams. https://en.wikipedia.org/wiki/
Robin_Williams

Richard Branson. https://en.wikipedia.org/wiki/
Richard_Branson

Buzz Aldrin. https://en.wikipedia.org/wiki/Buzz_Aldrin

Arnold Schwarzenegger. https://en.wikipedia.org/wiki/
Arnold_Schwarzenegger

Leo Durocher. <https:/en.wikipedia.org/wiki/
Leo_Durocher>

Lee Iacocca. https://en.wikipedia.org/wiki/Lee_Iacocca

Franklin D. Roosevelt. https://en.wikipedia.org/wiki/
Franklin_D._Roosevelt

Diana, Princess of Wales. https://en.wikipedia.org/wiki/
Diana,_Princess_of_Wales

George Halas. https://en.wikipedia.org/wiki/
George_Halas

Knute Rockne. https://en.wikipedia.org/wiki/
Knute_Rockne

Jack Dempsey. https://en.wikipedia.org/wiki/
Jack_Dempsey

Audrey Hepburn. https://en.wikipedia.org/wiki/
Audrey_Hepburn

Bill Clinton. https://en.wikipedia.org/wiki/Bill_Clinton

Mother Teresa. https://en.wikipedia.org/wiki/Mother_Teresa

Richard Nixon. https://en.wikipedia.org/wiki/Richard_Nixon

Additional Sources

www.brainyquote.com

www.positivelypositive.com

www.quotes.net

www.famousquotesandauthors.com

www.goodreads.com

Carnegie, Dorothy, *Dales Carnegie's Scrapbook*. New York: Dale Carnegie & Associates, Inc., 1959.

Hickman, Martha Whitmore, *Healing After Loss*. New York: Harper Collins Publishers, 1994.

About the Author

Ronald J. Avery is the youngest of eight children born and raised in Dubuque, Iowa. He attended Catholic grade school, high school, and college. He had a career in management of retail grocery for twenty-five years and management of wholesale beer for five years. He has had the pleasure of working with several thousand employees in his thirty years of management. He is now retired from retail and wholesale business to take up his passion in life, helping cancer patients. He is the founder, president, CEO and COB of the Avery Foundation based in Dubuque, Iowa. This Foundation gives grants to local cancer patients going through treatments. A portion of the sale of this book goes to the Foundation. For more information about the Avery Foundation, visit their website, averyfndtn.org.

CPSIA information can be obtained
at www.ICGtesting.com
Printed in the USA
LVHW100324010522
717404LV00001B/5